The
&
Church
&
Rituals
&
Handbook

THE
&
CHURCH
&
RITUALS
&
HANDBOOK

Jesse C. Middendorf

Beacon Hill Press of Kansas City
Kansas City, Missouri

Copyright 1997
by Beacon Hill Press of Kansas City

ISBN 083-411-6278

Printed in the
United States of America

Cover Design: Mike Walsh

+Congregation standing
*Optional or as time allows
**Where desired, lectionary selections may be utilized according to the calendar
STTL Hymnal, *Sing to the Lord* (Kansas City: Lillenas Publishing Company, 1993)
Note: Copies of services and rituals may be made for use of participants in worship, for this purpose only, without permission. Copies must be destroyed following use.

Library of Congress Cataloging-in-Publication Data
The church rituals handbook / compiled by Jesse C. Middendorf.
    p. cm.
  ISBN 0-8341-1627-8
    1. Church of the Nazarene—Liturgy—Texts.   2. Holiness churches—Liturgy—Texts.   3. Rites and ceremonies—Handbooks, manuals, etc.   I. Middendorf, Jesse.
  BX8699.N35C48   1997
  264'.0799—dc21   97-12067
                                                 CIP

10 9 8 7 6 5 4 3 2 1

To
Susan,
my wife, my friend,
my partner in ministry,
and to
Jesse A. and Martha Middendorf
who daily live the grace
embodied in ritual.

CONTENTS

CHURCH DEDICATIONS

OTHER RITUALS

INTRODUCTION

Time was when Evangelical Christians let their fear of formality and dread of the liturgical churches rob them of the meaning and blessing of holy rituals. We seemed to view liturgics, sacraments, and ceremonies the way that Augustine looked at sex in marriage—as a sort of lilac scented blasphemy that God in His mercy somehow permitted.

But we have outgrown that now, and we seek ways to embody our theology in rituals that add meaning to the landmarks on the corporate Christian journey.

We learned from the way that our formless conduct of worship took on its own dry predictable form (three songs, prayer, an offering or two, special song, and a long cliché-ridden sermon).

We learned the need for theologically based rituals from the singing of course country ballads at funerals (the deceased's favorite song).

We learned from trying to conduct weddings for which teenagers in the throes of passion insisted on writing their own ceremonies for troth plighting, sometimes with Communion—for the bride and groom only—tossed in as a nod to religion.

We learned from observing that appropriate ritual adds meaning and depth to the worship experience for contemporary Christians. If the event—Holy Communion, installation of a pastor, or dedication of a baby—requires a theologically-precise and congregationly-approved ritual, it ministers more grace than an off-the-cuff ad-lib between the announcements of the chili supper and the film on family finance.

We learned by noting that we need more ceremonies in which the congregation participates. When the whole community of faith participates in the baptism of the child, promising to minister to it and model the faith before it, the event becomes an act of the family of faith. When a convert is received into membership with affirmation and participation of the whole congregation, he or she becomes in a special way a child of the church. The rituals in this book accent the participation of the whole family of faith.

We have learned from the proclivity of evangelical religion

to become too individualistic. We believe that religion is a personal matter of the heart. But it is more than a "just me and You, Jesus, affair." A solitary Christian is an oxymoron. Maria Harris in her book *Fashion Me a People,* makes a significant point, saying that "We come to God together or we do not come at all." The creator of this book understands what Harris meant and offers us rituals that acknowledge the objective and corporate dimensions of the Christian faith.

You will note that the rituals in this book are public ceremonies. Unlike cults and secret orders, all Christian rituals—baptism, Communion, marriage, dedications, ordinations—are public affirmations or celebrations.

While serving on a denominational committee charged with editing the *Manual* for the Church of the Nazarene, we noticed that the Christian rituals there were not only written with typical evangelical simplicity but also downright sparse, some nearly bare. They had remained for decades virtually untouched and unrefined. The committee of Jack Stone, Alex Deasley, Richard Spindle, Wesley Tracy, and Jesse Middendorf noted how "user unfriendly" these typical evangelical rituals were. They commissioned one of the members to create a new edition of rituals that would be enriched by Christian tradition but also be characterized by enhanced communication to the contemporary Christian and congregation.

From a background of distinguished service as a pastor and churchman, Dr. Jesse Middendorf has put together these rituals that every pastor and congregation, I believe, will find to be faithful to the heritage and relevant to the times.

For ministers and congregations who use the *Manual of the Church of the Nazarene,* it may be helpful to note that the rituals for baptism, the reception of church members, the Lord's Supper, marriage, the funeral service, installation of officers, and church dedications are correlated with the 800 series of paragraphs in that source. (See page 237.)

As you use these rituals may Christ come to your family of faith spilling the light from His hands, speaking grace, and anchoring all in the bedrock of His redeeming love.

Wesley D. Tracy
April 1997

The Sacrament of Baptism

THE BAPTISM OF BELIEVERS

AN EXTENDED SERVICE OF CHRISTIAN BAPTISM

THE BAPTISM OF INFANTS OR YOUNG CHILDREN

THE DEDICATION OF INFANTS OR YOUNG CHILDREN

THE DEDICATION OF INFANTS OR YOUNG CHILDREN
(Ritual for Single Parent or Guardian)

THE SACRAMENT OF BAPTISM

The Baptism of Believers

DEARLY BELOVED: Baptism is the sign and seal of the new covenant of grace, the significance of which is attested by the apostle Paul in his letter to the Romans as follows:

"Know ye not, that so many of us as were baptized into Jesus Christ were baptized into his death? Therefore we are buried with him by baptism into death: that like as Christ was raised up from the dead by the glory of the Father, even so we also should walk in newness of life. For if we have been planted together in the likeness of his death, we shall be also in the likeness of his resurrection" (Rom. 6:3-5).

The earliest and simplest statement of Christian belief, into which you now come to be baptized, is the Apostles' Creed, which reads as follows:

"I believe in God the Father Almighty, Maker of heaven and earth;

"And in Jesus Christ, His only Son, our Lord; who was conceived by the Holy Ghost, born of the Virgin Mary, suffered under Pontius Pilate, was crucified, dead, and buried; He descended into hell; the third day He rose again from the dead;

He ascended into heaven, and sitteth at the right hand of God the Father Almighty; from thence He shall come to judge the quick and the dead.

"I believe in the Holy Ghost, the holy Church of Jesus Christ, the communion of saints, the forgiveness of sins, the resurrection of the body, and the life everlasting."

Will you be baptized into this faith? If so, answer, "I will."

Response: I will.

Do you acknowledge Jesus Christ as your personal Savior, and do you realize that He saves you now?

Response: I do.

Will you obey God's holy will and keep His commandments, walking in them all the days of your life?

Response: I will.

The minister, giving the full name of the person and using the preferred form of baptism—sprinkling, pouring, or immersion—shall say:

_____, I baptize thee in the name of the Father, and of the Son, and of the Holy Spirit. Amen.

An Extended Service of Christian Baptism

The following service order may be followed where a more expansive service is desired.

GATHERING
Prelude

INTRODUCTION TO THE SERVICE

As candidates for baptism come forward, an appropriate hymn of worship or testimony may be sung.

When the candidates are in place, the minister may make the following statement to the congregation:

DEAR FRIENDS: Through the sacrament of baptism, our entrance into the Body of Christ through the new birth is given visible expression. Having been incorporated into God's mighty act of salvation in Christ, we follow Him in baptism, publicly identifying with Him and testifying to our having appropriated by faith the benefits of the atonement that Christ has provided us in His suffering, death, and resurrection.

We join these persons in a celebration of the grace of God in their lives and unite our hearts in praise to the Father, the Son, and the Holy Spirit.

PRESENTATION OF THE CANDIDATES

A representative of the congregation presents the candidates to the minister and the congregation with appropriate statements:

I present _____ for baptism.

Proclamation of the Word or Testimony of Candidates

At this point in the service, a sermon regarding the significance of baptism may be preached, or the candidates may give a personal testimony to their Christian faith and experience. Where a small class of candidates is presented or time permits, both may be included.

Renunciation of Sin and Profession of Faith

The vows of Christian baptism have consisted, from the earliest periods of the Church, in a personal renunciation of sin and profession of faith. The minister may here address the candidates and ask them for their avowals of faith and obedience as follows:

On behalf of Christ and the Church, I ask you:

Do you renounce Satan and all the spiritual forces of wickedness that rebel against God?

Response: I renounce them.

Do you renounce the evil powers of this world that corrupt and that destroy the creatures of God?

Response: I renounce them.

Do you renounce sinful desires that draw you from the love of God?

Response: I renounce them.

Have you repented of your sins, turned to Christ, and accepted Him as your Savior?

Response: I have.

Have you put your whole trust in His grace alone for your redemption?

Response: I have.

Do you promise to follow and obey Him as your redeeming Lord?

Response: I do.

After the candidates have responded, the minister addresses the congregation, saying:

Will you who witness these vows do all in your power to support *these persons* in *their* life in Christ? Will you pray for them, encourage them, instruct and lead them, and will you so live before them that they may follow your example in Christian living?

People: We will.

The minister then says these or similar words to the congregation and the candidates:

Let us join *those* who *are* following Christ in baptism and reaffirm our faith.

Minister: Do you believe in God the Father?

People: I believe in God, the Father Almighty, Creator of heaven and earth.

Minister: Do you believe in Jesus Christ, the Son of God?

People: I believe in Jesus Christ, His only Son,

our Lord, who was conceived by the Holy Spirit, born of the Virgin Mary, suffered under Pontius Pilate, was crucified, dead, and buried; He descended to the dead; the third day He rose again from the dead; He ascended into heaven, and sitteth at the right hand of God the Father Almighty; from thence He shall come to judge the living and the dead.

Minister: Do you believe in God the Holy Spirit?

People: I believe in the Holy Spirit, the holy Church universal, the communion of saints, the forgiveness of sins, the resurrection of the body, and the life everlasting.

Minister: Will you continue in the apostles' teaching and fellowship, in the breaking of bread, and in prayer?

People: I will, with God's help.

Minister: Will you continue in resisting evil, and, should you fall into sin, will you repent and turn to the Lord?

People: I will, with God's help.

Minister: Will you proclaim by word and example the good news of God in Christ?

People: I will, with God's help.

Minister: Will you earnestly seek to purify yourself from everything that contaminates body and spirit, perfecting holiness out of reverence for Christ?

People: I will, with God's help.

Minister: Will you serve the present age, fulfilling in your life and ministry the call of Christ to make disciples of all nations?

People: I will, with God's help.

BAPTISM OF CANDIDATES

Candidates are ushered to the water by sponsors or congregational assistants. The chosen mode of baptism is administered, the minister using the given name of the candidate as follows:

_____, I baptize you in the name of the Father and of the Son and of the Holy Spirit. Amen.

WELCOME OF THE NEWLY BAPTIZED BY THE CONGREGATION

Pastor: Let us welcome the newly baptized.

People: We receive you into the household of God. Confess the faith of Christ crucified, proclaim His resurrection, and share with us in His eternal priesthood.

DOXOLOGY

BENEDICTION

The Baptism of Infants or Young Children

The original ritual for "The Baptism of Infants" appeared in the *Manual of the Church of the Nazarene* from 1908 to 1968. It was utilized as the only ritual regarding infants or young children until 1936. At that time a ritual for "The Dedication of Infants or Young Children" was added, along with the original rite for "The Baptism of Infants." In 1972 the ritual for "The Baptism of Infants" was removed from the *Manual,* and language for baptism was edited into the ritual for "The Dedication of Infants or Young Children." In 1980 a new ritual for "The Baptism of Young Children" was included in the ritual portion of the *Manual,* and the combination language was removed from the ritual for "The Dedication of Infants or Young Children."

While there are those within the Wesleyan-Holiness tradition who disagree with the practice of infant baptism in favor of "believers' baptism," those who support infant baptism do so in the belief that there is scriptural, theological, and historical warrant for the practice.

There are New Testament scriptures that make reference to the baptism of "households," implying the inclusion of all the members of the family, according to the interpretations of many scholars (Acts 16:15, 33; 1 Cor. 1:16). "Household baptisms, strengthened by such adjectives as *holos* (whole) and *pas* (all) and *hapartes* (entire, a strengthened form of *pas*), strongly imply that infants were baptized in these instances. Families were solidarities then, and the decisions of the father settled important matters for all others members of the family. This had long obtained in Judaism, and it obtained in the Gentile community of the first century."[1]

The Church of the Nazarene gives clear expression to its belief that young children are covered under the Atonement. The article of faith in the *Manual* on the Atonement (6) states: "The Atonement is graciously efficacious for the salvation of the irresponsible and for the children in innocency but is efficacious for the salvation of those who reach the age of responsibility only when they repent and believe."[2] It is certain that God's prevenient grace is already at work in the life of a young child, which gives warrant to the practice of infant baptism as a declaration of this prevenient grace.

And infant baptism further declares the covenant relationship that exists between Christ and the Church on the basis of the Atonement. Children who are baptized are included in the covenant community, declared in public rite to have been included in the finished work of Christ on the Cross. As one theologian has put it, "As a sacrament, baptism is not a purely personal matter between an individual and God. It is a sacrament of the Church. This means that the baptized person belongs to a fellowship. Christ came to overcome human isolation (1 John 1:3), and Christian life can be meaningful only in the fellowship of others. In baptizing infants, the Church is saying that the child is included in the fellowship, is a part of the Body, is under the covenant."[3]

H. Ray Dunning goes on to say, "Furthermore, a genuine validity can be attached to infant baptism if it is seen as the induction of the child into the covenant community with a concomitant commitment of the community to help guide the child 'in the nurture and admonition of the Lord' (Eph. 6:4, KJV). It might, in fact, militate against the loss of children from the church by guarding against the church becoming spectators until the child experiences an adult conversion."[4]

Theologians within the Wesleyan-Holiness tradition have given wide acknowledgment to the theological validity of infant baptism. Familiar names such as Wakefield, Wiley, Grider, Dunning, and Staples have expressed the significance of the practice and given theological rationale from a wide array of perspectives. Each has also appealed to the historical precedence, many citing evidences of the practice among the apostles and certainty of its inclusion in church practice before the end of the third century.

Perhaps the most eloquent expression of the intent of infant baptism is in the words of Dr. Rob Staples:

From the moment of baptism, as the baptized child grows and develops toward maturity, the parents and the Church are under solemn obligation to use every means available to communicate to the young person this Good News: "When you were too young to walk, we carried you in our arms. Likewise when you were too young to choose to be a part of the Body of Christ, we chose for you. We brought you into the fellowship, and you were incorporated into the Body. Now you will need to decide whether you will choose for yourself that which was chosen for you. We pray that you will choose it and not reject it."[5]

Knowing that it is not our faith but God's grace that saves us, in baptism, both for infants and believers, we celebrate God's prior grace toward us. Only secondarily and consequentially do we show through baptism our active response to God.

Having that confidence, the Wesleyan-Holiness tradition has embraced the practice of infant baptism, and the following rituals are included for the use of those parents who desire this sacred rite.

Included in this format is a suggested introduction to the rite of infant baptism that might be read in those churches who are less familiar with the practice. It expresses both the confidence that the ritual has significance to the church as well as the child and the expressed desire for the church to accept its responsibility to assist the child in his or her growth toward spiritual maturity and a personal affirmation of faith in Christ as the source of our redemption.

Following are both the original ritual for "The Baptism of Infants" and the later ritual for "The Baptism of Young Children." Following the rituals for baptism of children will be found the current *Manual* rituals for "The Dedication of Infants or Young Children."

The following introduction may be utilized where a congregation is unfamiliar with the ritual of infant baptism, giving a brief background for the practice, and a rationale for its place in the life of an evangelical congregation.

The Church has always understood the necessity for parents to make important choices for the spiritual welfare and development of their children. Among those is the choice of whether to offer their children to God in infant dedication or to request the pastor to administer the sacrament of infant baptism to their children. Many churches hold that either is an appropriate choice, but that the parents should make the decision with the counsel and guidance of family and pastor.

For those who choose infant baptism, many churches hold that there is a significant moment of grace involved, not that we convey grace in the sacrament, but that we proclaim the prevenient grace of God that covers this child from the time of birth, and even before. It is a symbol of the covenant that exists between God and the Church. In this rite we are indicating that we believe that God has incorporated this child into His Body by prevenient grace. But we are not determining for this child what his choices will be later in life.

There will come a time when these parents must say to this child, "When you were too young to walk, we carried you in our arms. Likewise, when you were too young to choose to be a part of the Body of Christ, we chose for you. We brought you into the fellowship, and you were incorporated into the Body. Now you will need to decide whether you will choose for yourself that which was chosen for you. We pray that you will choose it, and not reject it."[6]

When an infant or young child has been baptized, it is right and necessary that when they come to maturity, they be led to make their own very personal confession in Christ.

But today we celebrate that God in His prevenient grace has embraced this child in the covenant He has made with His people. We, as the people of God, have an obligation to nurture his (her) growth toward maturity and a personal love for Christ. This is God's child, and we are responsible for telling him (her) that as he (she) grows to maturity and accountability. Then, when he (she) is able to make the choice for himself (herself), he (she) may choose to embrace Christ by personal faith and continue in that grace.

Join me now as we participate in this sacred rite of baptism of a child.

Rite One

The family is invited to join the ministers at the front of the sanctuary, the child in the arms of a parent. The minister, facing the family and the congregation, shall read the following:

DEARLY BELOVED: Baptism is the external seal of the new covenant of grace. In presenting this child for Christian baptism, you must remember that it is your part and duty to see that he (she) be taught, as soon as he (she) shall be able to learn, the nature and the end of this holy sacrament. You shall call upon him (her) to give reverent attendance upon appointed means of grace; see that he (she) is taught the truth of God as contained in the Holy Scriptures, and help him (her) as you may be able in the way of life.

The minister may then ask the friends of the child to name the child and baptize it, saying:

_____, I baptize thee in the name of the Father, and of the Son, and of the Holy Ghost. Amen.

The minister may offer prayer, the congregation uniting in the Lord's Prayer.

Rite Two

When the sponsors shall have presented themselves with the child (or children) the minister shall say:

DEARLY BELOVED: While we do not hold that baptism imparts the regenerating grace of God, we do believe that Christ gave this holy sacrament as a sign and seal of the new covenant. Christian baptism signifies for this young child God's gracious acceptance on the basis of His prevenient grace in Christ, and points forward to his (her) personal appropriation of the benefits of the Atonement when he (she) reaches the age of moral accountability and exercises conscious saving faith in Jesus Christ.

In presenting this child for baptism you are hereby witnessing to your own personal Christian faith and to your purpose to guide him (her) early in life to a knowledge of Christ as Savior. To this end it is your duty to teach him (her), as soon as he (she) shall be able to learn, the nature and end of this holy sacrament; to watch over his (her) education, that he (she) may not be led astray; to direct his (her) feet to the sanctuary; to restrain him (her) from evil associates and habits; and as much as in you lies, to bring him (her) up in the nurture and admonition of the Lord.

Will you endeavor to do so by the help of God? If so, answer, "I will."

The minister may then ask the parents or guardians to name the child and shall then baptize the child, repeating his (her) full name and saying:

_____, I baptize thee in the name of the Father and of the Son and of the Holy Spirit. Amen.

The minister may then offer the following prayer or may use an extemporary prayer.

Heavenly Father, we humbly pray that Thou wilt take this child into Thy loving care. Abundantly enrich him (her) with Thy heavenly grace; bring him (her) safely through the perils of childhood; deliver him (her) from the temptations of youth; lead him (her) to a personal knowledge of Christ as Savior; help him (her) to grow in wisdom, and in stature, and in favor with God and man, and to persevere therein to the end. Uphold the parents with loving care, that with wise counsel and holy example they may faithfully discharge their responsibilities to both this child and to Thee. In the name of Jesus Christ our Lord. Amen.

The Dedication of Infants or Young Children

When the parents or guardians have presented themselves with the child (or children) the minister shall say:

"Then were there brought unto him little children, that he should put his hands on them, and pray; and the disciples rebuked them. But Jesus said, Suffer little children, and forbid them not, to come unto me; for of such is the kingdom of heaven" (Matt. 19:13-14).

In presenting this child for dedication you signify not only your faith in the Christian religion but also your desire that he (she) may early know and follow the will of God, may live and die a Christian, and come unto everlasting blessedness.

In order to attain this holy end, it will be your duty, as parents (guardians), to teach him (her) early the fear of the Lord, to watch over his (her) education, that he (she) be not led astray; to direct his (her) youthful mind to the Holy Scriptures and his (her) feet to the sanctuary; to restrain him (her) from evil associates and habits; and, as much as in you lies, to bring him (her) up in the nurture and admonition of the Lord.

Will you endeavor to do so by the help of God? If so, answer, "I will."

Pastor: I now ask you, the congregation; will

you commit yourself as the Body of Christ to support and encourage these parents as they endeavor to fulfill their responsibilities to this child and to assist _____ by nurturing his (her) growth toward spiritual maturity?

Response: We will.

Pastor: Our loving Heavenly Father, we do here and now dedicate _____ in the name of the Father, and of the Son, and of the Holy Spirit. Amen.

Then the minister may offer the following prayer or may use an extemporary prayer.

Heavenly Father, we humbly pray that Thou wilt take this child into Thy loving care. Abundantly enrich him (her) with Thy heavenly grace; bring him (her) safely through the perils of childhood; deliver him (her) from the temptations of youth; lead him (her) to a personal knowledge of Christ as Savior; help him (her) to grow in wisdom, and in stature, and in favor with God and man, and to persevere therein to the end. Uphold the parents with loving care, that with wise counsel and holy example they may faithfully discharge their responsibilities both to this child and to Thee. In the name of Jesus Christ our Lord. Amen.

The Dedication of Infants or Young Children

Ritual for Single Parent or Guardian

When the parent or guardian has presented himself (herself) with the child (or children) the minister shall say:

"Then were there brought unto him little children, that he should put his hands on them, and pray; and the disciples rebuked them. But Jesus said, Suffer little children, and forbid them not, to come unto me; for of such is the kingdom of heaven" (Matt. 19:13-14).

In presenting this child for dedication you signify not only your faith in the Christian religion but also your desire that he (she) may early know and follow the will of God, may live and die a Christian, and come unto everlasting blessedness.

In order to attain this holy end, it will be your duty, as a parent (guardian), to teach him (her) early the fear of the Lord, to watch over his (her) education, that he (she) be not led astray; to direct his (her) youthful mind to the Holy Scriptures, and his (her) feet to the sanctuary; to restrain him (her) from evil associates and habits; and, as much as in you lies, to bring him/her up in the nurture and admonition of the Lord.

Will you endeavor to do so by the help of God? If so, answer, "I will."

Response: I will.

Pastor: I now ask you, the congregation; will you commit yourself as the Body of Christ to support and encourage this parent as he (she) endeavors to fulfill his (her) responsibilities to this child and to assist _____ by nurturing his (her) growth toward spiritual maturity?

Response: We will.

Pastor: Our loving Heavenly Father, we do here and now dedicate _____ in the name of the Father, and of the Son, and of the Holy Spirit. Amen.

Then the minister may offer the following prayer or may use an extemporary prayer:

Heavenly Father, we humbly pray that Thou wilt take this child into Thy loving care. Abundantly enrich him (her) with Thy heavenly grace; bring him (her) safely through the perils of childhood; deliver him (her) from the temptations of youth; lead him (her) to a personal knowledge of Christ as Savior; help him (her) to grow in wisdom, and in stature, and in favor with God and man, and to persevere therein to the end. Uphold the parent with loving care, that with wise counsel and holy example he (she) may faithfully discharge his (her) responsibilities both to this child and to Thee. In the name of Jesus Christ our Lord. Amen.

The Reception of Church Members

THE RECEPTION OF CHURCH MEMBERS

The prospective members having come forward to stand before the altar of the church, the pastor shall address them as follows:

DEARLY BELOVED: The privileges and blessings that we have in association together in the Church of Jesus Christ are very sacred and precious. There is in it such hallowed fellowship as cannot otherwise be known.

There is such helpfulness with brotherly watch care and counsel as can be found only in the Church.

There is the godly care of pastors, with the teachings of the Word; and the helpful inspiration of social worship. And there is cooperation in service, accomplishing that which cannot otherwise be done.

The doctrines upon which the church rests as essential to Christian experience are brief.

We believe in God the Father, Son, and Holy Spirit. We especially emphasize the deity of Jesus Christ and the personality of the Holy Spirit.

We believe that human beings are born in sin; that they need the work of forgiveness through Christ and the new birth by the Holy Spirit; that subsequent to this there is the deeper work of heart cleansing or entire sanctification through the infilling of the Holy Spirit, and that to each of these works of grace the Holy Spirit gives witness.

We believe that our Lord will return, the dead shall be raised, and that all shall come to final judgment with its rewards and punishments.

Do you heartily believe these truths? If so, answer, "I do."

Response: I do.

Then the minister shall ask:

Do you acknowledge Jesus Christ as your personal Savior, and do you realize that He saves you now?

Response: I do.

Desiring to unite with the Church of the Nazarene, do you covenant to give yourself to the fellowship and work of God in connection with it, as set forth in the General Rules and Special Rules of the Church of the Nazarene? Will you endeavor in every way to glorify God, by a humble walk, godly conversation, and holy service; by devotedly giving of your means; by faithful attendance upon the means of grace; and, abstaining from all evil, will you seek earnestly to perfect holiness of heart and life in the fear of the Lord?

Response: I will.

The minister shall then say to the person or persons:

I welcome you into this church, to its sacred fellowship, responsibilities, and privileges. May the great Head of the Church bless and keep you, and enable you to be faithful in all good works, that your life and witness may be effective in leading others to Christ.

The minister shall then take each one by the hand, and with appropriate words of personal greeting welcome each into the church.

Alternate form for members joining by letter of transfer:

_____, formerly a member (members) of the Church of the Nazarene at _____, comes (come) to join the fellowship of this local congregation.

Taking each by the hand, or speaking to the group, the minister shall say:

It gives me pleasure on behalf of this church to welcome you into our membership. We trust that we will be a source of encouragement and strength to you and that you, in turn, will be a source of blessing and help to us. May the Lord richly bless you in the salvation of souls and in the advancement of His kingdom.

The Sacrament of the Lord's Supper

THE SACRAMENT OF THE LORD'S SUPPER

Rite One

The administration of the Lord's Supper may be introduced by an appropriate sermon and the reading of 1 Cor. 11:23-29; Luke 22:14-20, or some other suitable passage. Let the minister then give the following invitation:

The Lord himself ordained this holy sacrament. He commanded His disciples to partake of the bread and wine, emblems of His broken body and shed blood. This is His table. The feast is for His disciples. Let all those who have with true repentance forsaken their sins, and have believed in Christ unto salvation, draw near and take these emblems, and, by faith, partake of the life of Jesus Christ, to your soul's comfort and joy. Let us remember that it is the memorial of the death and passion of our Lord; also a token of His coming again. Let us not forget that we are one, at one table with the Lord.

The minister may offer a prayer of confession and supplication, concluding with the following prayer of consecration:

Almighty God, our Heavenly Father, who of Thy tender mercy didst give Thine only Son, Jesus

Christ, to suffer death upon the Cross for our redemption: hear us, we most humbly beseech Thee. Grant that, as we receive these Thy creatures of bread and wine according to the holy institution of Thy Son, our Savior Jesus Christ, in remembrance of His passion and death, we may be made partakers of the benefits of His atoning sacrifice.

We are reminded that in the same night that our Lord was betrayed, He took bread and, when He had given thanks, He broke it and gave it to His disciples, saying, "Take, eat: this is My body, which is broken for you: do this in remembrance of Me" (1 Cor. 11:24). Likewise, after supper, He took the cup, and when He had given thanks, He gave it to them, saying, "Drink ye all of this, for this is My blood of the New Testament, which is shed for you and for many, for the remission of sins" (Matt. 26:27-28); "do this, as oft as ye shall drink it, in remembrance of Me" (1 Cor. 11:25).

May we come before Thee in true humility and faith as we partake of this holy sacrament. Through Jesus Christ our Lord. Amen.

Then may the minister, partaking first, with the assistance of any other ministers present, and when necessary, of the stewards, administer the Communion to the people.

While the bread is being distributed, let the minister say:

The body of our Lord Jesus Christ, which was broken for you, preserve you blameless, unto everlasting life. Take and eat this, in remembrance that Christ died for you.

As the cup is being passed, let the minister say:

The blood of our Lord Jesus Christ, which was shed for you, preserve you blameless unto everlasting life. Drink this, in remembrance that Christ's blood was shed for you, and be thankful.

After all have partaken, the minister may then offer a concluding prayer of thanksgiving and commitment (33.5, 413.3, 413.10, 427.7, 429.1, *Manual,* Church of the Nazarene, 1993-97).

Rite Two

The following more detailed order of service may be utilized when desired:

A Service of Word and Table

Service of the Word

Prelude

Leader: O worship the LORD in the beauty of holiness;

People: Let the whole earth stand in awe of Him.

All: "Almighty God, unto whom all hearts are open, all desires known, and from whom no secrets are hidden: Cleanse the thoughts of our hearts by the inspiration of Your Holy Spirit, that we may perfectly love You and worthily magnify Your holy name; through Jesus Christ our Lord. Amen."

Processional*

+Hymn

Old Testament Lesson:

Appropriate lesson selected to coincide with the significance of the service or the meaning of the Passover as it is related to the sacrifice of Christ**

Hymn*

Psalm:

A selected psalm, portion of a psalm, or other Old Testament wisdom literature, perhaps arranged as a responsive reading for congregational participation**

EPISTLE LESSON:

Appropriate lesson selected to coincide with the significance of the service or the meaning of the Lord's Supper**

HYMN*

+GOSPEL LESSON:

Appropriate lesson selected to coincide with the significance of the service or the meaning of the Lord's Supper**

SERMON:

THE NICENE CREED:

If desired, the Apostles' Creed may be used

All: "We believe in one God, the Father, the Almighty, Maker of heaven and earth, of all that is, seen and unseen.

We believe in one Lord, Jesus Christ, the only Son of God, eternally begotten of the Father, God from God, Light from Light, true God from true God, begotten, not made, of one Being with the Father. Through him all things were made. For us and for our salvation he came down from heaven: by the power of the Holy Spirit he became incarnate from the Virgin Mary, and was made man. For our sake he was crucified under Pontius Pilate; he suffered death and was buried. On the third day he rose again in accordance with the Scriptures; he ascended into heaven and is seated at the right hand of the Father. He will come again in glory to judge the living and the dead, and his kingdom will have no end.

We believe in the Holy Spirit, the Lord, the Giver of life, who proceeds from the Father and the Son. With the Father and the Son he is worshiped and glorified. He has spoken through the Prophets.

We believe in one holy catholic and apostolic Church. We acknowledge one baptism for the forgiveness of sins. We look for the resurrection of the dead and the life of the world to come. Amen."

PRAYERS OF THE PEOPLE

COMMUNITY LIFE AND ANNOUNCEMENTS

GIVING OF TITHES AND FREEWILL OFFERINGS

+THE DOXOLOGY

If desired, during the singing of the Doxology, the elements of the Lord's Supper may be brought to the table of the Lord in preparation for distribution. Once the elements are placed on the table, the congregation standing, the minister may lead the following:

Minister: The Lord be with you.

People: And also with you.

Minister: Lift up your hearts.

People: We lift them up to the Lord.

Minister: Let us give thanks to the Lord our God.

People: It is right to give God thanks and praise.

Minister: It is right and a good and joyful thing, always and everywhere to give thanks to You, Father Almighty, Creator of heaven and earth. Grant to us, Lord, we pray, the spirit to think and do always the things that are right, that we, because we cannot exist without You, may be enabled to live according to Your will; through Jesus Christ, our Lord, who lives and reigns with You and the Holy Spirit, one God, now and forever. Amen.

All: Holy, holy, holy, Lord God of power and might, heaven and earth are full of Your glory. Hosanna in the highest. Blessed is he who comes in the name of the Lord. Hosanna in the highest.

Congregation may be seated

PRAYER OF CONSECRATION:

The minister may pray extempore, or the following may be used:

Minister: We acclaim You, holy Lord, glorious in power. Your mighty works reveal Your wisdom and love. You formed us in Your own image, giving the whole world into our care, so that we might serve all Your creation. When our disobedience took us far from You, You did not abandon us to the power of death. In Your mercy You came to our help, so that in seeking You we might find You. Through the prophets You taught us to hope for salvation. You sent Your only Son to be our Savior. And, that we might no longer live for ourselves, but for Him who died and was raised for us, You sent the Holy Spirit, Christ's first gift for those who believe, to complete His work in the world and to bring to fulfillment the sanctification of us all.

The minister, placing a hand on the bread, may pray:

When the hour had come for Him to be glorified by You, Heavenly Father, our Lord Jesus Christ took bread; and when He had given thanks to You, He broke it, and gave it to His disciples, and said, "Take, eat: this is my body, which is broken for you: this do in remembrance of me" (1 Cor. 11:24).

Placing a hand on the cup, the minister may pray:

After supper He took the cup of wine; and when He had given thanks, He gave it to them and said, "Drink from it, all of you. This is my blood of the covenant, which is poured out for many for the forgiveness of sins" (Matt. 26:27-28,

NIV). "Do this, whenever you drink it, in remembrance of me" (1 Cor. 11:25, NIV).

Minister: Therefore, according to His command, O Father,

People: We remember His death, we proclaim His resurrection, we rejoice in His gift of the Holy Spirit.

Minister: Lord, we pray that in Your goodness and mercy, Your Holy Spirit may descend upon us, and upon these gifts, sanctifying them and showing them to be holy gifts for Your holy people, the bread of life and the cup of salvation, the body and blood of Your Son, Jesus Christ.

Grant that all who share this bread and cup may become one body and one spirit, a living sacrifice in Christ, to the praise of Your name.

All this we ask through Your Son, Jesus Christ. By Him and with Him and in Him, in the unity of the Holy Spirit all honor and glory is Yours, Almighty Father, now and forever. Amen.

And now, as our Savior Christ has taught us, we pray:

All: Our Father, who art in heaven, hallowed be thy name. Thy kingdom come, thy will be done, on earth as it is in heaven. Give us this day our daily bread. And forgive us our trespasses, as we forgive those who trespass against us. And lead us not into temptation, but deliver us from evil. For thine is the kingdom and the power and the glory for ever. Amen (see Matt. 6:9-13).

If desired, the minister may hold a piece of the unleavened bread and cup of the juice of the vine and say:

Minister: Christ our Passover is sacrificed for us.

People: Therefore, let us keep the feast. Alleluia!

Minister: The gifts of God for the people of God. Take them in remembrance that Christ died for you, and feed on Him in your hearts by faith with thanksgiving.

All who confess Jesus Christ as Lord are welcome to come to His table.

Methods of serving the elements of the Lord's Supper vary. The congregation may be invited to the altar of the church, to be served by the elders of the church, assisted by others as prescribed in church polity.

The elements may be served by distributing trays containing the bread and wine to the seated congregation.

The elements may be served by the method of intinction. In this method, the minister stands at the altar or the table, holding a tray with pieces of unleavened Communion bread in one hand and a chalice or cup of juice of the grape in the other. The congregation files before the minister, each participant taking a piece of the bread and dipping it into the cup, and then eating the bread. The participant may then either kneel for a time at the altar or return to the pew for meditation and prayer while others are being served.

After all who desire to participate have been served, the minister shall continue.

Minister: Let us pray.

All: "Almighty and ever living God, we thank You for feeding us with the spiritual food of the body and blood of Your Son, our Savior Jesus Christ; and for assuring us that we are living members of His body. And now, Father, send us out to do the work You have given us to do, to love and serve You as faithful witnesses of Christ our Lord. To Him, to You, and to the Holy Spirit, be honor and glory, now and forever. Amen."

+HYMN

RECESSIONAL*

BENEDICTION: Now "may the God of peace . . . sanctify you entirely; and may your spirit and soul and body be kept sound and blameless at the coming of our Lord Jesus Christ. The one who calls you is faithful, and he will do this" (1 Thess. 5:23-24, NRSV). Amen.

POSTLUDE

Communion Under Special Circumstances

This form is intended for use when there are those who are not able, because of health or other extenuating circumstances, to participate in the Communion of the Lord's Supper with the congregation.

When persons are unable to participate with the congregation for extended periods of time, it is desirable that the pastor or other appropriate minister designee arrange to celebrate the Lord's Supper with them on a regular basis, wherever it is best suited to meet needs of the participants.

This form, or the form found in Rite One, would be appropriate for use.

When possible, members of the family, relatives, or friends from the congregation may be invited to join in the celebration of the Lord's Supper.

The celebration may begin with the following:

Almighty God, unto whom all hearts are open, all desires known, and from whom no secrets are hidden: Cleanse the thoughts of our hearts by the inspiration of Your Holy Spirit, that we may perfectly love You and worthily magnify Your holy name; through Jesus Christ our Lord. Amen.

The minister may read a passage of Scripture from the Gospel and other scriptures deemed appropriate for the occasion. One of the following may be read:

John 3:16

John 6:35

John 6:51, 55-56

John 15:4-5, 8-9

After reading the scriptures, the minister may comment on them briefly.

The minister may then pray a prayer of confession and supplication. The following may be used:

Father of Grace and Mercy, we come humbly before You in preparation for our participation in the holy sacrament of the Lord's Supper. We come in grateful recognition of Your love for us, as demonstrated in the gift of Your Son, Jesus Christ, for our redemption.

We humbly remember how we lived apart from Your grace, resisting Your love, and deserving nothing of Your mercies. And yet You extended Your gracious provision for our redemption through the suffering of Your Son, Jesus Christ, our Lord.

Grant to us a renewed appreciation for Your mercies. May the sufferings of Jesus on our behalf be embraced with faith and thanksgiving by all who are here. And may Your Holy Spirit accomplish in us that which is pleasing and acceptable to You, through Jesus Christ our Lord who, with You and the Holy Spirit, reigns in heaven and on earth, one God, Father, Son, and Holy Spirit. Amen.

If desired, the minister may invite those present to pray the Lord's Prayer, as follows:

Let us pray in the words our Savior Christ has taught us:

"Our Father, who art in heaven, hallowed be thy name. Thy kingdom come, thy will be done, on earth as it is in heaven.

"Give us this day our daily bread. And forgive us our trespasses, as we forgive those who trespass against us.

"And lead us not into temptation, but deliver us from evil.

"For thine is the kingdom and the power and the glory for ever. Amen" (see Matt. 6:9-13).

The minister may then pray a prayer of consecration of the elements of the sacrament. The following may be used if desired:

Heavenly Father, by Your mercy You gave Your only Son, Jesus Christ, to endure the sufferings on Calvary for our redemption. Hear us, we pray, that these emblems of bread and wine may become for us the representations of His body and blood, that we may be partakers of the benefits of His atoning sacrifice on our behalf.

We remember that in the same night that He was betrayed, our Lord took bread and, when He had given thanks, broke it and gave it to His disciples, saying, "Take, eat: this is my body, which is broken for you: this do in remembrance of me" (1 Cor. 11:24). In like manner, after supper, He took the cup, and when He had given thanks, He gave it to them, saying, "Drink from it, all of you. This is my blood of the covenant, which is poured out for many for the forgiveness of sins" (Matt. 26:27-28, NIV). "Do this, whenever you drink it, in remembrance of me" (1 Cor. 11:25, NIV).

May we come before You in true humility and faith as we partake of this holy sacrament. Through Jesus Christ our Lord. Amen.

The minister may say the following invitation:

The gifts of God for the people of God.

And may add:

Take them in remembrance that Christ died for you, and feed on Him in your hearts by faith with thanksgiving.

The sacrament is administered with the following or other words:

The body (blood) of our Lord Jesus Christ, given for you. His grace keep you in everlasting life. [Amen.]

Or:

The body (blood) of our Lord Jesus Christ, which was given for you, preserve you blameless unto everlasting life. Take this in remembrance that Christ suffered for you, and be thankful.

After the sacrament is served, words of benediction may be said or the following:

Gracious Father, we give You praise and thanks for this Holy Communion of the body and blood of Your Son, Jesus Christ our Lord, the means of our redemption. We pray that the mercies of God may produce in us a grateful heart that finds expression through holy living and perfect love to God and to people. Through Jesus Christ our Lord. Amen.

Matrimony

CHRISTIAN MARRIAGE

Christian marriage is a sacred and public covenant between a man and a woman in the presence of God. In the Church of the Nazarene, the marriage ceremony is administered by an elder or, where the laws of the state do not prohibit, a district licensed minister who is a pastor. It is required that the marriage be attested by at least two witnesses and that it conform to the laws of the state and the requirements of the church.

A couple presenting themselves for marriage should be required to participate in premarital counseling. They shall give assurance to the officiating minister of their understanding of the biblical standard of the permanence and inviolability of the marriage covenant.

The service of Christian marriage should be conducted as a service of the worship of God and may include the reading and proclamation of the Word and music that is appropriate to Christian worship.

Holy Communion may or may not be celebrated. In services where it is desired, its meaning should be made clear. Given the meaning and significance of Holy Communion, not only should the elements be served to the bride and groom, but also the congregation should be invited to participate. There should be no pressure that would embarrass anyone present who for whatever reason does not choose to receive the elements.

The decision to perform the ceremony of Christian marriage is the responsibility of the pastor, and all requirements of the state and the church shall be fulfilled. All plans for the conduct and content of the ceremony shall be approved by the pastor. Any policies and guidelines established by the congregation regarding decorations, photography, and audio or video recording of the ceremony should be communicated by the pastor or designee during consultation and preparation for the service. Decisions regarding music content and style should be made in consultation with the pastor. Music selections should be consistent with the nature of the sacred rite and reflect Christian values and customs.

Cultural or ethnic traditions consistent with the theological stance of the church may be incorporated into the service at the discretion of the pastor.

Rite One

At the day and time appointed for the solemnization of matrimony, the persons to be married—having been qualified according to the laws of the church and of the state, and by careful counsel and guidance by the minister—standing together, facing the minister, the man to the minister's left and the woman to the right, the minister shall address the congregation as follows:

DEARLY BELOVED: We are gathered together here in the sight of God, and in the presence of these witnesses, to join together this man and this woman in holy matrimony, which is an honorable estate, instituted of God in the time of man's innocency, signifying unto us the mystical union that exists between Christ and His Church. This holy estate Christ adorned and beautified with His presence and first miracle that He wrought, in Cana of Galilee, and St. Paul commended as being honorable among all men. It is, therefore, not to be entered into unadvisedly, but reverently, discreetly, and in the fear of God.

Into this holy estate these persons present now come to be joined.

Addressing the couple to be married, the minister shall say:

_____ and _____, I require and charge you both as you stand in the presence of God, to remember that the commitment to marriage is a commitment to permanence. It is the intent of God that your marriage will be for life, and that only death will separate you.

If the vows you exchange today be kept without violation, and if you seek always to know and do the will of God, your lives will be blessed with His presence, and your home will abide in peace.

Following the charge the minister shall say unto the man:

_____, will you have this woman to be your wedded wife, to live together after God's ordinance in the holy estate of matrimony? Will you love her, comfort her, honor and keep her in sickness and in health; and forsaking all others, keep yourself only unto her, so long as you both shall live?

Response: I will.

Then shall the minister say unto the woman:

_____, will you have this man to be your wedded husband, to live together after God's ordinance in the holy estate of matrimony? Will you love, honor, and keep him, in sickness and in health; and forsaking all others, keep yourself only unto him, so long as you both shall live?

Response: I will.

Then the minister shall ask:

Who gives this woman to be married to this man?

Response (by the father, or whoever gives the bride in marriage): I do (or Her mother and I).

[handwritten:) The CHANGE VOWS]

Facing each other and joining right hands, the couple shall then exchange the following vows:

The man shall repeat after the minister:

I, _____, take you, _____, to be my wedded wife, to have and to hold from this day forward, for better—for worse, for richer—for poorer, in sickness and in health, to love and to cherish, till death us do part, according to God's holy ordinance; and thereto I pledge you my faith.

[handwritten: I pledge you my faithfulness.]

The woman shall repeat after the minister:

I, _____, take you, _____, to be my wedded husband, to have and to hold from this day forward, for better—for worse, for richer—for poorer, in sickness and in health, to love and to cherish, till death us do part, according to God's holy ordinance; and thereto I pledge you my faith.

[handwritten: I pledge you my faithfulness.]

[handwritten: OPTIONAL RING SERVICE]

If desired, a ring ceremony may be inserted at this point. The minister receives the ring from the groomsman and, in turn, passes it to the groom. As he then places it upon the bride's finger, he shall repeat, after the minister:

This ring I give you as a token of my love and as a pledge of my constant fidelity.

[handwritten: GO TO UNITY CANDLE p. 82]

Repeat for double ring ceremony.

The couple then shall kneel as the minister offers the following, or an extemporaneous prayer:

O Eternal God, Creator and Preserver of all

mankind, Giver of all spiritual grace, the Author of everlasting life, send Thy blessing upon these Thy servants, this man and this woman, whom we now bless in Thy name; that as Isaac and Rebekah lived faithfully together, so these persons may surely perform and keep the vow and covenant made between them this hour and may ever remain in love and peace together, through Jesus Christ our Lord. Amen.

Then shall the minister say: ~~PRESENTATION~~ *DECLARATION, KISS, PRESENTATION*

Forasmuch as this man and woman have consented together in holy wedlock, and have witnessed the same before God and this company, and have declared the same by joining of hands, I pronounce that they are husband and wife together, in the name of the Father, and of the Son, and of the Holy Spirit. Those whom God has joined together let not man put asunder. Amen.

The minister shall then add this blessing:

God, the Father, the Son, and the Holy Spirit, bless, preserve, and keep you; the Lord mercifully with His favor look upon you, and fill you with all spiritual benediction and grace. May you so live together in this life that in the world to come you may have life everlasting.

The minister may then conclude with an extemporaneous prayer and/or benediction. (427.7, *Manual,* Church of the Nazarene)

Rite Two

GATHERING

As the people gather, instrumental or vocal music may be offered. Music used should be appropriate for Christian worship.

During the entrance of the wedding party, music may be instrumental, a congregational hymn may be sung, or a psalm, canticle, or anthem may be quoted or sung. The congregation may be invited to stand. The following processional hymns in *Sing to the Lord* are suggested:

"All Glory, Laud, and Honor," 215
"Christ Is Made the Sure Foundation," 671
"Come, Thou Almighty King," 3
"Joyful, Joyful, We Adore Thee," 17
"O God, Our Help in Ages Past," 95
"Praise, My Soul, the King of Heaven," 42
"Praise to the Lord, the Almighty," 20
"We're Marching to Zion," 389

The woman and the man may enter separately or together as the processional is engaged, accompanied by members of the wedding party. The woman and the man may be escorted by representatives of their families until they have reached the front of the church. Representatives of the families may be seated at this time or may stand with the couple through the Response of the Families, then be seated.

GREETING

Pastor to the congregation:

DEAR FRIENDS, we are gathered together in the sight of God to witness and to bless the joining together of _____ and _____ in Christian marriage. The covenant of marriage was established by God in creation when He created us male and female for each other.

Christ himself affirmed the beauty and significance of marriage with His presence and first miracle at the marriage in Cana of Galilee. Its permanence and inviolability were affirmed by Paul, who spoke with reverence of marriage as a demonstration of the relationship that Christ has with His Church. It is therefore to be entered into only with the most serious and lifelong commitment to each other's good in a union of strength, sympathy, and delight.

_____ and _____ come to give themselves to one another in this holy covenant.

DECLARATION OF INTENTION

The minister says to the persons who are to marry:

I ask you now, in the presence of God and these people, to declare your intention to enter into union with one another under the Lordship of Jesus Christ, who called you to himself and who has led you each to the other.

Minister to the woman:

_____, will you have _____ to be your husband, to live together with him in the covenant of marriage? Will you love him, comfort him, honor and keep him, in sickness and in health, and forsaking all others, be faithful to him as long as you both shall live?

Woman: I will.

Minister to the man:

_____, will you have _____ to be your wife, to live together with her in the covenant of marriage? Will you love her, comfort her, honor and keep her, in sickness and in health, and forsaking all others, be faithful to her as long as you both shall live?

Man: I will.

RESPONSES OF THE FAMILY AND CONGREGATION

Minister to the family:

The marriage of _____ and _____ unites their families and creates a new one. They ask your blessing on their union.

Parents and other representatives of the families may respond in one of the following ways:

We rejoice in your love for one another, and we pray God's blessing upon you.

Or the following:

Minister: As representatives of the families of _____ and _____, do you rejoice in their union, and do you pray God's blessing upon them?

Family members:

We do.

Minister to congregation:

Will you who witness the promises _____ and

_____ have made to one another do all in your power to uphold these two persons in their marriage? If so, please answer, "We will."

Congregation: We will.

PRAYER

The minister may pray extempore or may offer the following prayer:

Eternal God, Source and Creator of all things, and Fountain of all love, grant Your grace to _____ and _____. May the years ahead find them faithful to the vows they make today, and may the strength of the Holy Spirit enable them to grow together in the love, joy, and peace of our Savior Jesus Christ. Amen.

PROCLAMATION AND RESPONSE

Here a hymn, anthem, or other music may be offered and appropriate scripture may be read in preparation for proclamation.

SERMON OR READING WITNESSING TO CHRISTIAN MARRIAGE

PRAYER OF INTERCESSION FOR THE COUPLE

The minister may offer a prayer extempore, or the following may be prayed by the minister or by the congregation:

God of grace and glory, Giver and Preserver of all life, Source of mercy:
Bless and protect _____ and _____, through the power and presence of Your Holy Spirit.

May the vows they exchange be empowered by Your presence, and may the love of Christ be the source of their love for one another.

Enable them to grow in love and peace, their lives reflecting to each other the purity that finds its pattern in the love Christ has for His Church.

Grant that their lives may be filled with compassion and sensitivity to each other, and to the needs of the world around them. May their service to others be pleasing to You, and may they find joy in extending Your love and grace to others through Jesus Christ our Lord. Amen.

The Marriage

EXCHANGE OF VOWS

The man and woman face each other and join hands. The minister prompts them as necessary in exchanging these vows:

Man to woman:

In the name of God, I, _____, take you,
_____, to be my wife,
to have and to hold
from this day forward,
for better, for worse,
for richer, for poorer,
in sickness and in health,
to love and to cherish.

Death alone shall separate us.
   According to God's Holy Word,
I pledge you my faith and loyalty.

Woman to man:

In the name of God, I, _____, take you,
   _____, to be my husband,
  to have and to hold
from this day forward,
  for better, for worse,
for richer, for poorer,
  in sickness and in health,
to love and to cherish.

Death alone shall separate us.
   According to God's Holy Word,
I pledge you my faith and loyalty.

BLESSING AND EXCHANGE OF RINGS

The exchange of rings is optional. Where preferred, other symbols may be given instead of rings.

The minister, upon receiving the rings from the bearer, may say one of the following:

These rings are the outward and visible sign of an inward and spiritual grace, signifying to us the joining of _____ and _____ in holy marriage.

The minister may then bless the rings with an extempore prayer or the following:

Most Holy God, bless these rings *(this ring, these symbols)*. Grant that they who wear them may be faithful to each other and may be constant in their love for each other to their lives' end, through Jesus Christ our Lord. Amen.

The minister gives each ring in turn to the couple. While placing the ring on the third finger of the recipient's left hand, the giver may say (prompted by the minister):

_____, I give you this *ring* as a symbol of my love,
and with all that I am and all that I have,
I commit myself to you;
in the name of the Father and of the Son and of the Holy Spirit. Amen.

BLESSING OF THE MARRIAGE

The husband and wife may kneel as the minister prays:

O Eternal God, You have so honored the covenant of marriage that in it is found the demonstration of the covenant between Christ and His Church. You have so constituted it that it is entered into for as long as this life shall last.

_____ and _____ entered this covenant willingly with the purpose that their lives may grow in godliness and love, and that their home shall be a haven of grace and peace. May they keep their covenant of love for one another as faithfully as You have kept Your covenant of love with us. And may the power of Your Holy Spirit empower them for keeping their promises in all the years to come. Amen.

Declaration of Marriage

> The husband and wife join hands. The minister may place a hand on their joined hands.

Now that _____ and _____ have given themselves to each other through the exchange of vows, by the joining of hands, and by the giving and receiving of rings, I pronounce that they are husband and wife together, in the name of the Father and of the Son and of the Holy Spirit. Those whom God has joined together in marriage, let no one ever separate. Amen.

> If Holy Communion is to be celebrated, the service continues with the Thanksgiving and with the elements offered to all the congregation. The service order may follow the order of service found in this handbook, "The Sacrament of the Lord's Supper" Rites One and Two, or as indicated in the following section. A marriage ceremony in which Holy Communion is celebrated may best be facilitated by providing a written order of worship for the congregation.

> If Holy Communion is not to be celebrated, the service continues with the following Prayer of Thanksgiving:

Most gracious God, Creator and Preserver of all people, we give You thanks for Your love and tenderness.

You have made us a covenant people through our Savior Jesus Christ and have demonstrated Your grace in bringing together these two people whose love we celebrate this day.

May Christ's love purify their love for each other, and may His presence keep them sensitive to the needs of the other.

Let their love be a demonstration of Your love to the world around them, and honor their service to others as service to You.

Bless them in their work and in their companionship; in their waking and in their sleeping; in their sorrows and in their joys; in their living and in their dying.

At last, may their lives be crowned by the approval You grant them, that they may join us all at that table where Your saints feast forever in Your heavenly home; through Jesus Christ our Lord, who with You and the Holy Spirit lives and reigns, one God, for ever and ever. Amen.

THANKSGIVING AND COMMUNION

(See instructions for serving Holy Communion in this handbook.)

Minister: The Lord be with you.

People: And also with you.

Minister: Lift up your hearts.

People: We lift them to the Lord.

Minister: Let us give thanks to the Lord our God.

People: It is right to give Him thanks and praise.

It is right, and a good and joyful thing, always and everywhere to give thanks to You, Father Almighty, Creator of heaven and earth.

Because in the love of wife and husband, You have given us an image of the heavenly Jerusalem, adorned as a bride for her bridegroom, Your Son Jesus Christ our Lord; who loves her and gave himself for her, that He might make the whole creation new.

And so, with Your people on earth and all the company of heaven, we praise Your name and say,

"Holy, holy, holy Lord, God of power and might, heaven and earth are full of Your glory. Hosanna in the highest. Blessed is he who comes in the name of the Lord. Hosanna in the highest."

Holy are You, and blessed is Your Son Jesus Christ, whom You sent in the fullness of time to be a light to the world. In the new covenant established in His blood is the image for the covenant love of husband and wife.

On the night in which He gave himself for us, He took bread, gave thanks to You, broke the bread, gave it to His disciples, and said: "Take, eat: this is my body, which is broken for you: this do in remembrance of me" (1 Cor. 11:24).

When the supper was ended, He took the cup, gave thanks to You, gave it to His disciples, and said: "Drink from it, all of you. This is my blood of the covenant, which is poured out for many for the forgiveness of sins" (Matt. 26:27-28, NIV). "Do this, whenever you drink it, in remembrance of me" (1 Cor. 11:25, NIV).

And so, in remembrance of these Your mighty acts in Jesus Christ, we offer ourselves in praise and thanksgiving as a holy and living sacrifice, in union with Christ's offering for us, as we proclaim the mystery of faith.

"Christ has died, Christ is risen, Christ will come again."

Pour out Your Holy Spirit on us, gathered here, and on these gifts of bread and wine. Make them be for us the body and blood of Christ, that we may be for the world the Body of Christ, redeemed by His blood.

Bless _____ and _____ with Your Holy Spirit. May their love reflect the love Christ has for us, a love that is pure and strong.

By Your Spirit make them one with Christ, one with each other, and one in ministry to all the world, until Christ comes in final victory and we, with them, feast at His heavenly banquet.

Through Your Son Jesus Christ, with the Holy Spirit in Your holy Church, all honor and glory is Yours, Almighty Father, now and forever. Amen.

THE LORD'S PRAYER

Minister: And now, with these whom God has united in marriage, let us pray:

"Our Father, who art in heaven, hallowed be thy name. Thy kingdom come, thy will be done, on earth as it is in heaven. Give us this day our daily bread. And forgive us our trespasses, as we forgive those who trespass against us. And lead us not into temptation, but deliver us from evil. For thine is the kingdom and the power and the glory forever. Amen" (see Matt. 6:9-13).

BREAKING THE BREAD

The minister, standing behind the Lord's table facing the congregation, breaks the bread and then lifts the cup in silence or with appropriate words.

COMMUNION

The bread and wine are given to the congregation with appropriate words being exchanged. The husband and wife may assist in the distribution.

The body of Christ, given for you. Amen.
The blood of Christ, given for you. Amen.

While the bread and wine are given, the congregation may sing hymns, or there may be appropriate vocal or instrumental music.

When all have received, the Lord's table is put in order.

The minister may then offer prayer:

God of mercy and love,
You have brought _____ and _____ together along with this company of friends and family. We have feasted at Your table and rejoice in Your love.

Grant that these two servants of Yours may grow in love, in wisdom, and in spiritual strength. Crown their home with blessing and peace. May their living here please You and serve Your kingdom.

Through Jesus Christ our Lord. Amen.

BLESSING AND DISMISSAL

Minister to husband and wife:

God grant you the peace of Christ, the joy of service, and the wisdom of years. May His peace fill your home and His grace guide your going. Go to serve God and your neighbor in all that you do.

Minister to people:

Bear witness to the love of God in your world, and be filled with His Spirit in your words and your doing. The love of God, the grace of the Lord Jesus Christ, and the presence of the Holy Spirit be with you all. Amen.

The couple may greet each other with a kiss and be greeted by the pastor, after which greetings may be exchanged through the congregation.

A hymn may be sung or instrumental music played as the couple, the wedding party, and the people leave.

Rite Three

The following ceremony provides an alternative to the more frequently used ceremonies. Drawn from a variety of resources, it provides some options that may be utilized in planning a ceremony that highlights the centrality of worship in the rituals of the church.

GATHERING

While the people are gathering, music appropriate for Christian worship is played, utilizing vocal or instrumental music. During the Gathering, guests and family members are seated, and candles are lighted.

After guests and family are seated, the entrance of the wedding party is accompanied by a hymn, by an anthem, or by other appropriate music. The entrance of the grandparents and parents of the bride and groom signifies the beginning of the ceremony. Their order of entry is as follows: the groom's grandparents, the bride's grandparents, the groom's parents, the bride's mother.

After the grandparents and parents are seated, the order of entry of the wedding party is typically as follows: the ushers or groomsmen, bridesmaids, maid (unmarried woman)/matron (married woman) of honor, ring bearer(s), and flower girl(s).

The woman and the man, entering separately or together, now come forward with other members of the wedding party. The woman and the man may be escorted by representatives of their families (traditionally, the groom by his father or best man, and the bride by her father or other male family member) until they have reached the front of the church or through the Response of the Families, at which time the escort(s) (usually the bride's escort) is seated. The couple facing the minister, the minister facing the congregation, the ceremony continues.

GREETINGS

DEAR FRIENDS: We have come together in the presence of God to witness and to bless the joining of _____ and _____ in Christian marriage.

The covenant of marriage was established by God in creation and has been blessed through the ages by the people of God. Our Lord Jesus Christ blessed this manner of life with words of affirmation and instruction, and His presence and first miracle, at a marriage in Cana of Galilee.

Christian marriage signifies to us the beauty and mystery of the union that Christ has with His Church, and the Scripture commends it to be honored among all people.

The union of husband and wife in heart, body, and mind is intended by God for their mutual joy; for the help and comfort given each other in all seasons and conditions in life; and when God so provides, for the procreation of children and their nurture and training in the knowledge and love of God in Christ.

Christian marriage is therefore of great significance. It is not to be entered with haste or lack of careful thought and prayer but reverently, deliberately, and in careful accord with the purposes for which it is intended by God.

THE CHARGE TO THE MAN AND THE WOMAN

_____ and _____, as you stand before this gathered company of friends and family, and as you present yourselves to God, I charge you to remember that you enter into a covenant with each other that is patterned after the covenant of faithfulness God has established with us.

Your marriage is to be the object of your best endeavors. So live in loyalty and faithfulness to each other that your home becomes eloquent testimony to the character of your relationship with the Lord Jesus Christ. May He be the acknowledged Witness to your words and deeds, your thoughts and attitudes. May the quality of your life together be measured by the depth of your love for Him.

THE DECLARATION OF INTENT

The minister shall address the man as follows:

Will you, ＿＿＿＿＿＿, take ＿＿＿＿＿＿, to be your wife; and will you now promise, in the presence of God and before these gathered witnesses, to be a loving, faithful, and loyal husband to her, whatever may come, until God shall separate you by death?

The man shall answer:

I will.

The minister shall then address the woman as follows:

Will you, ＿＿＿＿＿＿, take ＿＿＿＿＿＿, to be your husband; and will you now promise, in the presence of God and before these gathered witnesses, to be a loving, faithful, and loyal wife to him, whatever may come, until God shall separate you by death?

The woman shall answer:

I will.

BLESSING OF THE COUPLE BY THE PARENTS OR FAMILIES

The minister may address the families of the bride and groom as follows:

_____, _____ *[names of families' members],* do you give your blessing to _____ and _____, and promise to do everything in your power to uphold them in their marriage?

The families may respond:

We rejoice in your union and pray God's blessing upon your home.

BLESSING OF THE COUPLE BY THE CONGREGATION

The minister may address the congregation as follows:

Dear friends of _____ and _____: You have come to witness this exchange of vows. Will you do in all your power to support this marriage now and in the years to come? If so, please answer, "We will."

The congregation shall answer:

We will.

PRAYER FOR ILLUMINATION

The minister may pray extemporaneously or pray the following:

O God of light and understanding, You show us

the way, the truth, and the life. You sustain us with
Your Holy Spirit. We take joy in Your presence with
us and pray for Your guidance and illumination as
we hear Your Word. May _____ and _____
find strength in this moment of openness to You.
Through Jesus Christ our Lord. Amen.

READING FROM SCRIPTURE

One or more scripture passages are read.

HOMILY

Suggested homilies are included in the *Manual* appen-
dix and may serve as models for developing of a homily
or may be used as printed.

Following the homily, an appropriate hymn or other response may be used.

The Marriage

EXCHANGE OF VOWS

The woman and the man face each other and join
hands. The minister may prompt them in the repeating of the vows to one another.

The man shall say to the woman:

I, _____, receive you, _____, as a gift
    from God,
  to be my lifelong companion.
I will love you through laughter and tears,
    through health and sickness,
    in plenty and in want,

at work and at play.
I will love you constantly and with the deepest
loyalty.
I will prayerfully seek your joy and happiness
throughout our lives. Amen.

The woman shall say to the man:

I, _____, receive you, _____, as a gift
from God,
to be my lifelong companion.
I will love you through laughter and tears,
through health and sickness,
in plenty and in want,
at work and at play.
I will love you constantly and with the deepest
loyalty.
I will prayerfully seek your joy and happiness
throughout our lives. Amen.

BLESSING AND EXCHANGE OF RINGS

The exchange of rings is optional. Other symbols may
be given in addition to or instead of rings.

The minister may say one of the following:

Most gracious God, in the time of Noah, You
gave the rainbow as a sign of promise. Bless
these symbols that they may also be signs of
promises fulfilled in the lives of these servants of
Yours, through Jesus Christ our Lord. Amen.

While placing the ring on the third finger of the recipient's left hand, the giver may say the following:

_____, I give you this ring as a sign of my vow, and with all that I am, and all that I have, I honor you; in the name of the Father and of the Son and of the Holy Spirit. Amen.

UNITY CANDLE

The lighting of a unity candle is a recently developed tradition in the wedding service. It is intended to symbolize the oneness that characterizes Christian marriage.

When a unity candle is desired, the two side candles, representing the husband and wife, are lighted early in the service, often by the mothers of the bride and groom while the family is being seated at the beginning of the service.

The center candle is lighted by the bride and groom after the exchange of vows and the exchange of rings. The side candles remain lighted to symbolize that each partner retains his or her personal identity while the two are united as husband and wife.

During the lighting of the unity candle, music may be played or sung.

An explanation of the symbolism of the candle may be given by the minister prior to the lighting. The minister may read one of the following:

The unity candle symbolizes that _____ and _____ are joined together as one flesh. They have become one and are intended to treat each other as if the other were a part of their own flesh.

The love that is characterized by this unity is best described by the words of Ruth to Naomi in the Old Testament: "Do not press me to leave you

or to turn back from following you! Where you go,
I will go; where you lodge, I will lodge; your peo-
ple shall be my people and your God my God.
~~Where you die, I will die—there will I be buried~~
(Ruth 1:16-17, NRSV).   *Go To Scripture & Homily p. 87*

Or:

"Then the man said, 'This at last is bone of my
bones and flesh of my flesh; this one shall be
called Woman, for out of Man this one was tak-
en.' Therefore a man leaves his father and his
mother and clings to his wife, and they become
one flesh" (Gen. 2:23-24, NRSV).

DECLARATION OF MARRIAGE

The wife and husband join hands and face the minister. The minister may place a hand on their joined
hands.

Pastor to bride and groom:

You have declared your vows and given symbols of your love before God and this congregation. May God confirm your covenant and fill you
both with His grace.

The couple may turn and face the congregation.

Pastor to people:

Now that _____ and _____ have given
themselves to each other by solemn vows, with
the joining of hands, (and the giving and receiving of rings,) I announce to you that they are

husband and wife; in the name of the Father and of the Son and of the Holy Spirit.

Those whom God has joined together, let no one ever separate.

The congregation may be invited to stand while a doxology or other appropriate hymn is sung.

THE BLESSING OF THE MARRIAGE

The groom and bride may kneel as the minister prays:

Eternal God, You have blessed the covenant of Christian marriage, investing in it the symbolism of the union that exists between Christ and His Church. On this holy union between _____ and _____ grant Your blessing and peace. May the testimony of their lives give joy to You, and may they find Your Holy Spirit empowering them to grow in love and likeness to Christ. May their home be a place of refuge and happiness for them both, and may the joy You take in them be seen in the blessings You bestow upon them. Through Jesus Christ our Lord. Amen.

If Holy Communion is to be celebrated, the congregation is invited to participate with the wedding party as the service continues with the Thanksgiving and Communion. (See the Service of Holy Communion section of this handbook.)

If Holy Communion is not to be celebrated, the service continues with a prayer of Thanksgiving given extemporaneously by the minister, or the following prayer may be read:

Gracious Father, accept our thanks for Your

making us a covenant people through Jesus Christ our Lord. And thank You for blessing _____ and _____ in the exchange of their vows of love and loyalty this day.

Grant that their love for each other may reflect the love of Christ for us, and may that love grow in them daily.

Honor their home with Your presence, and preserve their commitments with Your strength.

Bless their work and their service, and may they know the peace and prosperity both desire, which shall yield to You for Your purposes.

May their living be of such joy to You that they shall finally stand before You with assurance and be able to sit at the table with Your saints from all ages. Through Jesus Christ our Lord, who with You and the Holy Spirit lives and reigns for ever and ever. Amen.

DISMISSAL WITH BLESSING

Here a song or hymn may be sung.

Minister to bride and groom:

God the Father bless you and preserve you; Christ the Lord honor your vows with His peace; God the Holy Spirit fill you with His love, as you seek His will and do it.

Minister to congregation:

Bear witness to the love of God in this world, so that those to whom love is a stranger will find

it in your generous friends. The grace of the Lord
Jesus Christ and the love of God and the communion of the Holy Spirit be with you all. Amen.

> The couple may greet each other with a kiss. If desired,
> the minister may introduce the couple to the congrega-
> tion. A hymn may be sung or instrumental music may
> be played as the couple, the wedding party, and the
> people leave.

SUBSEQUENT MARRIAGE

> On occasion, ministers are asked to solemnize the mar-
> riage of persons who, as a result of death or divorce,
> are entering a subsequent marriage. If after careful
> counsel and in following the guidelines of the *Manual*
> a minister believes that the marriage fulfills the best
> of God's plan for the couple, the marriage should ad-
> dress the needs of any children who will live in the
> home. If desired, the children may be asked to partici-
> pate in the ceremony, and the following may serve as a
> model for their participation in a commitment to
> growth, stability, and peace in the home.

> The minister may address the children as follows:

Your parents have discovered in one another a
deep and abiding love. They have prayerfully
sought the will of God for themselves and for you
and desire that each of you be a vital part of this
family that God has brought together. They have
committed themselves to one another in marriage, believing it is best for them and for you.

Will you commit yourselves to seek to be a family that learns to love one another as Christ loves
us? (Where other living parents exist, the follow-

ing may be included if the couple desires to do so:) While there are other parents for whom you have, and should have, a deep and abiding love, will you seek to encourage and support your father (mother) in this marriage and allow God to bless this home with His grace and peace?

If, with God's help, you will do this, please answer, "I will."

Children: I will.

HOMILY:

Scripture: 1 Cor. 13

_____ and _____, those are words of great power and significance for you today. And as we, your family and friends, join you in the celebration of your marriage vows, we could wish for the two of you nothing greater than that your love would be characterized by the qualities described in that passage of Holy Scripture.

The apostle Paul gives us a powerful model for married love in these verses. Love's definition is seen in its most compelling description. You see, you must always remember that love is not a feeling you have; love is something you do! Oh, I am not saying you do not or should not feel deeply about your love and about the one you love. And the love each of you feels for the other is moving and deep. There is an emotional content to love that is very satisfying. But Paul reminds us here that when the emotional tone in your lives and in your marriage tends to ebb and flow, as it will from time to time, loving deeds and intentions must still be the foundation of your relationship.

Hear these words again: "Love is patient; love is kind; love is not . . . boastful . . . or rude. It does not insist on its own way; it is not irritable or resentful. . . . It bears all things," believes all the best of its object, and is enduringly hopeful (NRSV). Love, you see, is not determined by how you feel. It is the choice you make toward your beloved one.

In your love, make room for forgiveness. And in your forgiveness, make room for growth. Each of you must learn to forgive readily and to seek forgiveness readily. It will not always be easy, and it must never be one-sided. You will have plenty of reasons for forgiveness, but hopefully, each occasion will also be an occasion for growth, as persons and as a couple, in your relationship with each other and in your relationship with Christ. That is what Paul is saying to us.

Those are strong words! And they would be impossible to understand were it not that each of you has come to know, very personally, the One who is the Source of such love. The apostle Paul himself knew what you know as well. Love like that is patterned after and made possible only by Jesus Christ. The only way you can hope to offer to each other a love as pure and meaningful as that is when you know and understand the Source of that love. You cannot produce it on your own. It is the love of God himself poured into your life by the Holy Spirit, through Jesus Christ. It is yours when you have allowed Him to become Lord of life for each of you as persons and for you as a couple, as husband and wife.

My prayer for you both is that you will continue to allow this love to find its source, not in your ability to produce it, but in His ability to provide it in you and through you.

And remember this: Neither of you will be able to find in each other the ultimate source of love and meaning. That each of you must find only in Jesus Christ. But once you find your meaning and love in Him, you will be able to give love and meaning to the other. Find your ultimate fulfillment in Christ, and you will then be able to give fulfillment to each other.

_____ and _____, we, all of us who are here with you today, wish for you the very best of God's blessings. May your lives be filled with love as they are filled with Christ,

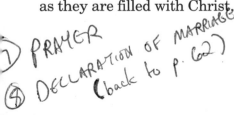

1) PRAYER
2) DECLARATION OF MARRIAGE
(back to p. 62)

The Funeral Service

THE FUNERAL SERVICE

DEARLY BELOVED: We are gathered today to pay our final tribute of respect to that which was mortal of our deceased loved one and friend. To you members of the family who mourn your loss, we especially offer our deep and sincere sympathy. May we share with you the comfort afforded by God's Word for such a time as this:

"Let not your heart be troubled: ye believe in God, believe also in me. In my Father's house are many mansions: if it were not so, I would have told you. I go to prepare a place for you. And if I go and prepare a place for you, I will come again, and receive you unto myself; that where I am, there ye may be also" (John 14:1-3).

"I am the resurrection, and the life: he that believeth in me, though he were dead, yet shall he live: and whosoever liveth and believeth in me shall never die" (John 11:25-26).

INVOCATION

In the minister's own words or the following:

Almighty God, our Heavenly Father, we come into this sanctuary of sorrow, realizing our utter dependence upon Thee. We know Thou dost love us and canst turn even the shadow of death into the light of morning. Help us now to wait before Thee with reverent and submissive hearts.

Thou art our Refuge and Strength, O God—a very present Help in time of trouble. Grant unto us Thy abundant mercy. May those who mourn today find comfort and healing balm in Thy sustaining grace. We humbly bring these petitions in the name of our Lord Jesus Christ. Amen.

A HYMN OR SPECIAL SONG

SELECTIONS OF SCRIPTURE

"Blessed be the God and Father of our Lord Jesus Christ, which according to his abundant mercy hath begotten us again unto a lively hope by the resurrection of Jesus Christ from the dead, to an inheritance incorruptible, and undefiled, and that fadeth not away, reserved in heaven for you, who are kept by the power of God through faith unto salvation ready to be revealed in the last time. Wherein ye greatly rejoice, though now for a season, if need be, ye are in heaviness through manifold temptations: that the trial of your faith, being much more precious than of gold that perisheth, though it be tried with fire, might be found unto praise and honour and glory at the appearing of Jesus Christ: whom having not seen, ye love; in whom, though now ye see him not, yet believing, ye rejoice with joy unspeakable and full of glory: receiving the end of your faith, even the salvation of your souls" (1 Pet. 1:3-9).

(Other passages that might be used are: Matt. 5:3-4, 6, 8; Pss. 27:3-5, 11, 13-14; 46:1-6, 10-11.)

MESSAGE

A HYMN OR SPECIAL SONG

CLOSING PRAYER

* * *

AT THE GRAVESIDE

When the people have assembled, the minister may
read any or all of the following scriptures:

"For I know that my redeemer liveth, and that
he shall stand at the latter day upon the earth:
and though after my skin worms destroy this
body, yet in my flesh shall I see God: whom I
shall see for myself, and mine eyes shall behold,
and not another" (Job. 19:25-27).

"Behold, I shew you a mystery; We shall not all
sleep, but we shall all be changed, in a moment,
in the twinkling of an eye, at the last trump: for
the trumpet shall sound, and the dead shall be
raised incorruptible, and we shall be changed. . . .
Then shall be brought to pass the saying that is
written, Death is swallowed up in victory. O
death, where is thy sting? O grave, where is thy
victory? The sting of death is sin; and the
strength of sin is the law. But thanks be to God,
which giveth us the victory through our Lord Jesus Christ.

"Therefore, my beloved brethren, be ye sted-
fast, unmoveable, always abounding in the work

of the Lord, forasmuch as ye know that your labour is not in vain in the Lord" (1 Cor. 15:51-52, 54-58).

"I heard a voice from heaven saying unto me, Write, Blessed are the dead which die in the Lord from henceforth: Yea, saith the Spirit, that they may rest from their labours; and their works do follow them" (Rev. 14:13).

The minister shall then read one of the following committal statements:

For a Believer:

Forasmuch as the spirit of our departed loved one has returned to God, who gave it, we therefore tenderly commit his (her) body to the grave in sure trust and certain hope of the resurrection of the dead and the life of the world to come, through our Lord Jesus Christ, who shall give to us new bodies like unto His glorious body. "Blessed are the dead which die in the Lord."

For a Nonbeliever:

We have come now to commit the body of our departed friend to its kindred dust. The spirit we leave with God, for we know the merciful Judge of all the earth will do right. Let us who remain dedicate ourselves anew to live in the fear and love of God, so that we may obtain an abundant entrance into the heavenly Kingdom.

For a Child:

In the sure and certain hope of the resurrection to eternal life through our Lord Jesus Christ, we commit the body of this child to the grave. And as Jesus, during His earthly life, took the children into His arms and blessed them, may He receive this dear one unto himself, for, as He said, "of such is the kingdom of heaven" (Matt. 19:14).

PRAYER

Our Heavenly Father, God of all mercy, we look to Thee in this moment of sorrow and bereavement. Comfort these dear ones whose hearts are heavy and sad. Wilt Thou be with them, sustain and guide them in the days to come. Grant, O Lord, that they may love and serve Thee and obtain the fullness of Thy promises in the world to come.

"Now the God of peace, that brought again from the dead our Lord Jesus, that great shepherd of the sheep, through the blood of the everlasting covenant, make you perfect in every good work to do his will, working in you that which is wellpleasing in his sight, through Jesus Christ; to whom be glory for ever and ever. Amen" (Heb. 13:20-21).

Installation Services

INSTALLATION OF PASTOR

INSTALLATION OF OFFICERS

INSTALLATION SERVICES

Installation of Pastor

The installation of a pastor is a sacred and significant event in the life of a congregation and in the life of the pastor. The process of searching for, nominating, electing, and installing a pastor offers opportunity for the congregation to reexamine its mission, reaffirm its core values, and anticipate the continuing leadership of the Holy Spirit in the ministry of the church to its community.

The opportunity to celebrate the beginning of a new relationship will strengthen the ties between pastor and people and should receive the highest attention by all concerned.

The district superintendent should be given opportunity to participate in the service, where possible, and may wish to be involved in the design of the service. Local leaders should plan the service well, using it as an opportunity to involve the widest possible number of people in relating to and installing the pastor as shepherd and overseer of the flock of God.

The following suggested order of service and ritual is designed to provide for meaningful interaction between platform leaders, the pastor, and the congregation. Careful attention should be given to every element of the service and adequate time given to prepare a meaningful and affirming service.

PRELUDE

PROCESSIONAL

PRAISE

Various hymns may be used to celebrate the leadership and faithfulness of God.

PRAYER

CREED

> The Apostles' Creed may be read in unison at this
> place in the service.

INSTALLATION OF PASTOR

Ceremony of Installation

PART I: INTRODUCTION (District Superintendent)

For 20 centuries now, in every generation, the
Church has set aside some of her members for
special training and preparation, ordaining
them to serve as clergy. She elects them to positions of responsibility, not privilege. They are to
serve the needs of the Church. These ministers
give up their lives, so to speak, for their lives are
not their own; they serve if and when and where
and in the capacities that the Church invites
them to serve. They are the servants of God. The
Early Church referred to them with words that
meant "table waiter," "under rower" (oarsman in
a large ship), "slave," "priestly servant," and
"shepherd." The Church ordains only those
whom she believes God has called to such service.

District Superintendent to New Pastor: Will
you accept the charge to be the spiritual leader of
this flock?

Pastor: I will.

District Superintendent to Congregation: Will you, the members of this church, accept, support, and uphold Rev. _____ as your pastor?

Congregation: We will.

PART II: INVITATION AND COVENANT FOR THE CHURCH

1. A Sunday School Teacher
Accept this Bible and be among us "a man (woman) of one book," as Mr. Wesley said be in this place one who proclaims the Word.

2. Member of Board of Stewards
Receive this vessel of water, the water of baptism. Be among us an evangelist who brings many to the knowledge of Jesus Christ as Lord and Savior, and to the affirmation of faith pronounced by the baptismal water.

3. Sanctuary Choir President
Receive this hymnal and be among us a leading worshiper at the foot of the Cross, that we may worthily magnify the name of God and our Savior, Jesus Christ.

4. A Young Family
Receive this directory containing a list of all our families. We are all your people. Pray for us, and be a priest and pastor among us that we might be acceptable to the Lord.

5. Member of Board of Stewards

Receive this oil, and be a healer and reconciler among us and a model of spiritual leadership to those of us training for ministry.

6. A Senior Couple

Accept this *Manual of the Church of the Nazarene* and the duty of teaching and discipling this people, reminding us that we are not only Christians but also Nazarene Christians.

7. The District Superintendent

Take this bread and cup and with it the authority to administer in Christ's stead the sacrament of Holy Communion among this people.

COVENANTAL LITANY

> Congregation led by secretary of the church board. Congregation standing.

Leader: Will you affirm that you believe that this pastor and this church are to be workers together in the providence of God?

People: This we do believe and affirm.

Leader: Will you support this pastor with respect, loyalty, love, and fervent prayer?

People: This we will do with God's help.

Leader: Will you receive the pastor's family members as members of our own family of faith, and love and pray for them as our own?

People: This we will do with God's help.

Leader: Will you give sacrificially of your means so that this pastor can be relieved of the temporal cares of this life so that he (she) may give his (her) full attention "to prayer, and to the ministry of the word" (Acts 6:4, KJV)?

People: This we will do with God's help.

Leader: Will you respond to pastoral leadership by vigorous participation in the congregational life of this church as it carries out its fourfold mission of worship, evangelism, nurture, and service?

People: This we will do with God's help.

Reading of the Word

Congregation seated.

A Church Board Member: "Here is my servant, whom I uphold, my chosen one in whom I delight; I will put my Spirit on him and he will bring justice to the nations. He will not shout or cry out, or raise his voice in the streets. A bruised reed he will not break, and a smoldering wick he will not snuff out. In faithfulness he will bring forth justice; he will not falter or be discouraged till he establishes justice on earth. In his law the islands will put their hope" (Isa. 42:1-4, NIV).

A Church Board Member: "This is what God the LORD says—he who created the heavens and stretched them out, who spread out the earth and all that comes out of it, who gives breath to its people, and life to those who walk on it: 'I, the LORD, have called you in righteousness; I will take hold of your hand. I will keep you and will make you to be a covenant for the people and a light for the Gentiles, to open eyes that are blind, to free captives from prison and to release from the dungeon those who sit in darkness'" (Isa. 42:5-7, NIV).

A Sunday School Teacher: "To each one of us grace was given according to the measure of Christ's gift. . . .

"He Himself gave some to be apostles, some prophets, some evangelists, and some pastors and teachers, for the equipping of the saints for the work of ministry, for the edifying of the body of Christ."

A Church Member: "Till we all come to the unity of the faith and the knowledge of the Son of God."

A Church Member: "To a perfect man, to the measure of the stature of the fullness of Christ."

A Church Member: "That we . . . speaking the truth in love, may grow up in all things into Him who is the head—Christ."

Congregation: "From whom the whole body, joined and knit together by what every joint supplies, according to the effective working by which every part does its share, causes growth of the body for the edifying of itself in love" (Eph. 4:7, 11-16, NKJV).

PART III: THE PASTOR'S COVENANT:✷

In response to the gracious call of God and in gratitude for the confidence you have expressed in me, I receive these symbols of pastoral leadership.

I pledge to you a stewardship of these resources and covenant with you to make ours a living, efficient church:

—a church in which sermon and sacrament are based strongly on the Word and enlivened with the dynamic presence of the Holy Spirit;

—a church with the atmospheric expectation of conversions;

—a church where the tempted are environed with victory;

—a church where the redeemed are enabled to see their larger need of Christ in cleansing fullness;

—a church where the particular consolations of God are given to the afflicted;

—a church where Christian men and women begin even on earth to be an authentic Christian community;

—a church that constantly bears toward the whole world with sacrifice in its heart and conquest in its purpose.

I pledge to you a stewardship of my responsibilities as pastor:

—to live before you with integrity and Christian simplicity;

—to responsibly administer the affairs of the church in consultation and cooperation with the church board, the church staff, and the people of the congregation as we carry out "the work of the ministry, for the edifying of the body of Christ."

—to lead you in worship as a worshiping leader, developing a careful regimen of study, prayer, reflection, and preparation, for the purposes of personal growth and ministry;

—to encourage you, comfort you, instruct and challenge you, by the preaching of the Word and the administration of the sacraments;

—to seek always and in all appropriate ways to expand the borders of the kingdom of God, cooperating with the district and general Church of the Nazarene in fulfilling a worldwide agenda;

—to live my family role responsibly, giving to each member the care and love due him (her) as a gift of God to me;

—to listen carefully to you, care deeply for you, work closely with you, and pray daily for you, that we may "grow up in all things into Him who is the head—Christ";

—to be a servant-leader, after the example of Christ.

PART IV: CHARGE TO PASTOR AND CHURCH

District Superintendent to the Pastor: Having committed yourself to this work, I charge you to care alike for the young and old, strong and weak, rich and poor. By your words and by your life proclaim the gospel of Jesus Christ.

District Superintendent to the Congregation: Since you have willingly and prayerfully called Pastor _____ to work among you, I charge you to willingly and prayerfully support, cooperate, and work together with him (her) in the name of Jesus Christ, whom you both serve.

PART V: MUTUAL COVENANT BETWEEN PASTOR AND PEOPLE

Pastor and people read in unison:

Congregation standing.

- We shall strive to cooperatively create and sustain an effective ministry that will renew and strengthen each member of this community of faith.
- We shall actively seek and welcome into membership all persons without regard to their economic or social status, race, or nationality.
- We shall accept our responsibility for moral

and spiritual development in our community, living by Christian standards of good citizenship.

- We shall work together with other churches and denominations in our community for the advancement of Christ's kingdom whenever we have the opportunity to do so.
- We shall periodically evaluate our church's fellowship and ministry in light of our mission.
- If problems present barriers to the mutual effectiveness of pastor and congregation, we shall cooperatively pray, faithfully communicate, and work in love to find solutions in the spirit of Christian understanding.
- We shall work to insure that our church appropriately relates itself to the mission, institutions, and doctrines of the Church of the Nazarene and the redemptive mission of Christ in our community, nation, and the world. Amen.

District Superintendent: By the power invested in me as superintendent of the _____ District of the Church of the Nazarene, I announce to you that having committed themselves to mutual covenants, Pastor _____ and the _____ Church of the Nazarene have entered a new and solemn relationship, that of pastor and people. Please greet your new senior pastor.

PRAISE SONG: "God's Faithfulness"

   Introduction of New Family by District Superintendent

OFFERTORY

DOXOLOGY

MINISTRY IN MUSIC

MESSAGE

RESPONSE

INVITATION TO RECEPTION

PRAYER

BENEDICTION

Installation of Officers

Following the singing of an appropriate hymn, let the
secretary read the names and positions of the officers
to be installed. These may come forward and stand at
the altar of the church, facing the minister. A covenant
card† should be provided for each. The minister shall
then say:

Recognizing God's method of setting apart certain workers for specific areas of Christian service, we come to this moment of installation of
these officers (and/or teachers) who have been
duly chosen to serve in our church for the ensu-
ing year. Let us consider God's instructions to us
from His Holy Word.

"I beseech you therefore, brethren, by the mercies of God, that ye present your bodies a living
sacrifice, holy, acceptable unto God, which is your
reasonable service. And be not conformed to this
world: but be ye transformed by the renewing of
your mind, that ye may prove what is that good,
and acceptable, and perfect, will of God" (Rom.
12:1-2).

"Study to shew thyself approved unto God, a
workman that needeth not to be ashamed, right-
ly dividing the word of truth" (2 Tim. 2:15).

"Let the word of Christ dwell in you richly in
all wisdom; teaching and admonishing one another in psalms and hymns and spiritual songs,

---

†Available from the Nazarene Publishing House.

singing with grace in your hearts to the Lord" (Col. 3:16).

"Let him that is taught in the word communicate unto him that teacheth in all good things" (Gal. 6:6).

We now come to this important moment when you who stand before the altar are to take upon yourselves the task of caring for the affairs of the church and its auxiliary organizations. May you look upon the assignments you now assume as special opportunities for service for our Lord, and may you find joy and spiritual blessing in the performance of your respective duties.

Yours is no light task, for the ongoing of the church and the destiny of souls are in your hands. The development of Christian character is your responsibility, and leading the unsaved to Jesus Christ is your highest objective. May God grant you wisdom and strength as you do His work for His glory.

You have been given a card on which is printed a covenant. We shall read it in unison, and as we do so, let us make it a personal commitment.

Worker's Covenant

Arrange before the service to have a card for each participant with the following printed on it:

In consideration of the confidence placed in me by the church in being selected for the office I now assume, I hereby covenant:

To maintain a high standard of Christian living and example in harmony with the ideals and standards of the Church of the Nazarene.

To cultivate my personal Christian experience by setting aside each day definite time for prayer and Bible reading.

To be present at the regular Sunday School, the Sunday morning and Sunday evening preaching services, and the midweek prayer meeting of the church, unless providentially hindered.

To attend faithfully all duly called meetings of the various boards, councils, or committees to which I have been, or will be, assigned.

To notify my superior officer if I am unable to be present at the stated time, or to carry out my responsibilities in this office.

To read widely the denominational publications and other books and literature which will be helpful to me in discharging the duties of my office.

To improve myself and my skills by participating in Continuing Lay Training courses as opportunity is afforded.

To endeavor to lead people to Jesus Christ by manifesting an active interest in the spiritual welfare of others and by attending and supporting all evangelistic meetings in the church.

The minister shall then offer an appropriate prayer, and a special song of dedication may be sung, after which the minister shall say:

Having pledged together your hearts and hands to the task of carrying forward the work of this church in your particular assignments, I herewith install you in the respective positions to which you have been elected or appointed. You are now a vital part of the organizational structure and leadership of this church. May you, by example, by precept, and by diligent service, be effective workers in the vineyard of the Lord.

The minister shall ask the congregation to rise and shall address them as follows:

You have heard the pledge and covenant entered into by your church leaders for the coming year. I now charge you, as a congregation, to be loyal in your support of them. The burdens which we have laid upon them are heavy, and they will need your assistance and prayers. May you always be understanding of their problems and tolerant of their seeming failures. May you lend assistance joyfully when called upon, so that, as we work together, our church may be an effective instrument in winning the lost to Christ.

The minister may then lead in a concluding prayer or have the congregation repeat the Lord's Prayer in unison.

Church Dedications

CHURCH DEDICATIONS

Rite One

The dedication of a new church building may be the occasion for a comprehensive dedication of the various components of the facility as well. The dedication of the facilities is most properly understood as the dedication of the people of the church to the proper use of those facilities, which are but the tools through which the church fulfills its mission.

A service of dedication for a new facility may provide occasion for the involvement of many people in the service, thereby broadening the sense of ownership of the objectives and the purposes for which the facility has been constructed or purchased.

The following ritual of dedication presupposes a wide participation of the people of the church and the occasion of dedicating a new facility as well as its furnishings. It is a comprehensive order of service as well as ritual of dedication.

PRELUDE

CALL TO WORSHIP

Pastor: "This is the day the LORD has made; let us rejoice and be glad in it" (Ps. 118:24, NIV).

People: "I was glad when they said unto me, Let us go into the house of the LORD" (Ps. 122:1).

Pastor: "This is none other than the house of God, and this is the gate of heaven" (Gen. 28:17, RSV).

People: The Lord is great beyond all telling; He exceeds all praise. Alleluia, Alleluia.

INVOCATION

The congregation is seated following the invocation.

THE LITURGY OF THE WORD

OLD TESTAMENT LESSON

Two or more readers may be utilized in the following reading.

Reader 1: Then King David rose to his feet and said, . . . "Solomon my son, acknowledge your father's God and serve him with whole heart and willing mind, for the LORD searches all hearts.

Reader 2: "If you search for him, he will let you find him, but if you forsake him, he will cast you off for ever. Remember, then, that the LORD has chosen you to build a house for a sanctuary: be steadfast and do it."

Reader 1: David ordered all the officers of Israel to help Solomon. . . . "Devote yourselves, therefore, heart and soul, to seeking guidance of the LORD your God, and set about building his sanctuary,

Reader 2: "So that the Ark of the Covenant of the LORD and God's holy vessels may be brought into a house built in honour of his name."

Reader 1: Solomon had finished the house of the Lord. . . . Then Solomon, standing in front of the altar of the LORD, in the presence of the whole assembly . . . , spread out his hands . . . and said,

Reader 2: "O LORD God of Israel, there is no god like thee in heaven or on earth, keeping covenant with thy servants and showing them constant love while they continue faithful to thee in heart and soul. . . . But can God indeed dwell with [mortals] on the earth? Heaven itself, the highest heaven, cannot contain thee; how much less this house that I have built!"

Reader 1: The LORD . . . said, "I have heard your prayer and I have chosen this place. . . . I have chosen and consecrated this house, that my Name may be there for all time and my eyes and my heart be fixed on it."

Unison: Except the LORD build the house, their labor is but lost that build it. This is the LORD's doing; it is marvellous in our eyes *(1 Chron. 28:2, 9-10; 22:17, 19; 2 Chron. 7:11; 6:12, 14, 18; 7:12, 16; see Pss. 127:1; 118:23, all NEB.)*

CONGREGATIONAL SONG: "All Glory, Laud, and Honor"

NEW TESTAMENT LESSON

Reader 1: But now in Christ Jesus you who once were far off have been brought near by the blood of Christ. . . . So then you are no longer

strangers, but . . . members of the household of
God, built upon the foundation of the apostles
and prophets, with Christ Jesus himself as the
[chief] cornerstone.

Reader 2: In him the whole structure is joined
together and grows into a holy temple in the
Lord. . . . In him you too are being built with all
the rest into a spiritual dwelling for God.

Reader 1: Therefore come to him, a living
stone, though rejected by mortals yet chosen and
precious in God's sight, and like living stones, let
yourselves be built into a spiritual house, . . . acceptable to God through Jesus Christ. For it
stands in scripture:

"See, I am laying in Zion a stone,

a cornerstone chosen and precious;

and whoever believes in him

will not be put to shame."

Reader 2: "The stone that the builders rejected
has become the very head of the corner." . . . The
household of God is the church of the living God,
the pillar and bulwark of the truth.

Unison: There can be no other foundation beyond that which is already laid; I mean Jesus
Christ himself *(Eph. 2:13, 19-21, NRSV; v. 22, NEB;
1 Pet. 2:4-6, 7; 1 Tim. 3:15, all NRSV; 1 Cor. 3:11,
NEB).*

WELCOME AND INTRODUCTIONS

PRESENTATION OF THE SANCTUARY

> Here the symbolic presentation of the keys to the building to the pastor by the chairperson of the Building Committee may be made. If the contractor is present, he or she may be asked to participate in the presentation as well.

DEDICATION OF THE SANCTUARY BUILDING
FOR THE WORSHIP OF THE HOLY TRINITY

Pastor: Beloved in the Lord, we rejoice that God has put it into the hearts of His people to build this house to the glory of His name. Let us now dedicate it to the worship of our God, Father, Son, and Holy Spirit, and to the service of all persons for whom Christ died.

To the worship of God the Father, who created us and loves us.

People: We dedicate this house.

Pastor: To the glory of God the Son, who redeemed us by His grace.

People: We dedicate this house.

Pastor: To the honor of the Holy Spirit, who sanctifies and guides us.

People: We dedicate this house.

DEDICATORY RESPONSE

> Here the district superintendent or pastor may briefly

respond to the dedication of the building with appropriate remarks.

DEDICATORY PRAYERS

PRAYER TO GOD THE FATHER

A member of the church board may be asked to read this prayer, expressed on behalf of the people.

Ever living Father, watchful and caring, our Creator and our End: All that we have and all that we are is Yours. Accept us now as we dedicate this place to which we come to praise Your name, to ask Your forgiveness, to know Your healing power, to hear Your Word, and to be nourished by the body and blood of Your Son. Be present always to guide and to judge, to illumine, and to bless Your people.

PRAYER TO GOD THE SON

A member of the congregation may be asked to read this prayer on behalf of the people.

Lord Jesus Christ, our Redeemer, make this a temple of Your presence and a house of prayer. Be always near us when we seek You in this place. Draw us to You, when we come alone and when we come with others, to find comfort and wisdom, to be supported and strengthened, to rejoice and give thanks. May it be here, Lord Christ, that we are made one with You and with one another, so that our lives are sustained and sanctified to Your service.

Prayer to God the Holy Spirit

A member of the congregation, perhaps a young person, could be asked to read this prayer on behalf of the congregation.

God, Holy Spirit, Sanctifier of the faithful, open our eyes, our ears, and our hearts that we may grow closer to You through joy and through suffering. Be with us in the fullness of Your power as new members are added to Your household, as we grow in grace through the years, when we are joined in marriage, when we turn to You in sickness or special need, and, at last, when we are committed into the Father's hands. O Father, Son, and Holy Spirit, whom we worship as one God, sanctify this place.

Congregational Song: "Holy, Holy, Holy"

Dedication of the Pulpit

Litany of Dedication

A member of the church board or the pastor may be asked to lead this portion of the litany.

Reader: Grant, O Lord, that Your holy Word will be faithfully read and preached from this sacred desk.

People: Your Word is a lamp to guide our feet.

Reader: Grant, O Lord, that the hearers of the gospel proclaimed here will understand what You are calling them to do and will receive the strength to answer the divine call.

People: Your Word is a light upon our path.

Reader: Grant, O Lord, that sinners will find salvation and believers will find the highway of holiness through the preaching that comes from this pulpit.

People: Your prophetic Word is a light that shines in a dark place, until the day dawns and the morning star rises in our hearts.

Reader: Grant, O Lord, that as the hungry and those wandering in darkness sit before this pulpit, they shall be fed the Bread of Life, and they shall see the Light of the World.

People: The unfolding of Your Word gives light and wisdom even to the simple and unlearned.

Reader: We dedicate this pulpit in the name of the Father, Son, and Holy Spirit.

People: Amen and alleluia.

DEDICATION OF THE ALTAR

A SEVENFOLD PRAYER OF DEDICATION

A member of the church or staff involved in evangelism may be asked to lead this portion of the litany.

Reader: O God, we now dedicate this altar as a place of prayer. From this day forward let those who would offer prayers of repentance for sin kneel here.

People: O God, when Your people sin against

You but then return to You with all their heart and soul, hear from heaven and forgive them.

Reader: Let those who would offer prayers of confession, of need, kneel here.

People: Our sins are higher than our head, our guilt has reached to the heavens.

Reader: Let those who would consecrate their lives to God kneel here.

People: By the mercies of God we present our bodies as a living sacrifice.

Reader: Let those in need of saving or sanctifying grace kneel here.

People: May the God of peace himself sanctify us through and through.

Reader: Let those who need courage, strength, and wisdom kneel here.

People: The fear of the Lord is the beginning of wisdom.

Reader: Let those who sorrow with groanings too deep for words kneel here.

People: The Spirit himself makes intercession for us with groanings which cannot be uttered.

Reader: Let those who before this altar are joined in holy matrimony kneel here.

People: What God has joined together let not mortals put asunder.

DEDICATION OF THE BAPTISTERY

PRAYER OF DEDICATION

The pastor or other congregational leader may read the prayer.

Grant, O Lord, that this baptistery, which we now hallow for Thy service, may powerfully symbolize the "washing of regeneration" to all those who shall be baptized therein. May they be truly washed and purified by the Holy Spirit. May they truly die unto sin and rise again unto righteousness, and always remain in the assembly of Your faithful children, through Jesus Christ our Lord.

People: There is one Lord, one faith, one baptism, one God and Father of all, to whom we dedicate this baptistery. Amen and alleluia.

DEDICATION OF THE TABLE OF THE LORD

The pastor may lead this portion of the litany.

The table of the Lord is, first of all, a symbol of redemption. Here we focus our worship upon the shed blood and broken body of our Lord, Jesus Christ. Each time we gaze upon it we are reminded that we are redeemed by His blood, saved by His grace.

We now hallow this table for the celebration of the sacrament of Jesus' broken body and shed blood. Whenever we see it, kneel before it, partake of its bread and wine, we will be reminded that He died for us, redeemed us by His blood, sustains us on our journey, and that He, the Bread of Life, is coming again.

People: This is the Bread which comes down from heaven; that one may eat thereof and not die.

CONGREGATIONAL SONG: "When I Survey the Wondrous Cross"

PRAYER OF DEDICATION

Pastor

Grant, O God, that whosoever shall receive at this table the blessed sacrament of the blood and body of Thy Son may receive all the benefits of His poured out love and grace. Give to the communicants a penitent heart, forgiveness for transgression, a fervent hope in Christ, confirmation of salvation, strength to carry out God's will, loyalty to the Church of Jesus Christ, an abiding love for others, and a treasured expectation for the coming again of our Lord. Through Jesus Christ our Lord. Amen.

CONSECRATION OF THE MUSIC FOR WORSHIP

The leader of music may lead this portion of the litany. The responses are taken from selected portions of 2 Chron. 5:11-14 and Ps. 126, usu. NRSV.

Leader: The priests came out of the holy place,

and all the levitical singers, their children and kindred with them, arrayed in fine linen, with cymbals, harps, and lyres.

People: Then our mouth was filled with laughter, and our tongue with shouts of joy.

Leader: The trumpeters and singers made themselves heard in unison in praise and thanksgiving to the LORD.

People: The LORD has done great things for us, and we rejoiced.

Leader: And when they raised with one voice the song:
"For he is good,
for his steadfast love endures forever,"
then the house, the house of the LORD,
was filled with a cloud; for the glory,
the glory of the LORD filled the house.

People: Those who sow in tears
shall reap in joy.
Those who go out weeping,
bearing precious seed,
shall come home with shouts of joy,
bringing with them their sheaves.

DEDICATORY RESPONSE

Here the director of music may briefly make appropriate remarks in receiving the facilities and furnishings for the music of worship.

PRAYER OF DEDICATION

Pastor

O God, Your people worship You with many voices and sounds, in times of joy and sorrow. Move us to express the wonder, the power, and the glory of Your creation and redemption in the music we make and in the songs we sing.

People: Praise God in His sanctuary.
Praise Him with the sound of the trumpet.
Praise Him with strings and pipe.
Praise Him according to His excellent greatness.
Amen and alleluia.

CHOIR

Suitable hymns or anthems would include "Christ Is Made the Sure Foundation" or "The Church's One Foundation." Following the music, the music leader and the congregation may be invited to read responsively as follows:

Leader: What a foundation we stand on now: the apostles and the prophets; and the cornerstone of the building is Jesus Christ himself! We who believe are carefully joined together with Christ as parts of a beautiful, constantly growing temple for God *(Eph. 2:20-21, TLB).*

People:
The Church's one foundation Is Jesus Christ, her Lord.
She is His new creation By water and the Word.

*From heaven He came and sought her To be His
     holy bride;*
*With His own blood He bought her, And for her
     life He died.*

*Yet she on earth hath union With God, the
     Three in One,*
*And mystic, sweet communion With those
     whose rest is won.*
*O happy ones and holy! Lord, give us grace that
     we,*
*Like them, the meek and lowly, On high may
     dwell with Thee.*

—Samuel J. Stone

THE DEDICATORY SERMON

THE DEDICATION OF THE PEOPLE OF GOD

You are God's building. Surely you know that
you are God's temple, where the Spirit of God
dwells. . . . The temple of God is holy; and that
temple you are.

Do you not know that your bodies are limbs
and organs of Christ? Do you not know that your
body is a shrine of the indwelling Holy Spirit,
and the Spirit is God's gift to you? . . . You are not
your own; you were bought with a price.

The temple of the living God is what we are.
God's own words are:

"I will live and move about among them;
I will be their God, and they shall be my people."

And therefore, ". . . Touch nothing unclean. . . .
I will be a father to you,
and you shall be my sons and daughters."
Therefore, . . . let us cleanse ourselves from all filthiness of the flesh and spirit, perfecting holiness in the fear of God *(1 Cor. 3:9, 16-17; 6:15, 19, all NEB; vv. 19-20, RSV; 2 Cor. 6:16-18, NEB; 7:1).*

PROCLAMATION OF DEDICATION

Pastor: We have dedicated this building and its contents. Yet we know that the true church is not made of brick and stone but people. Whatever else the church may be called, it is, according to the Scripture, a called-out community of faith.

God dwells with and within His people. They form His temple "not made with hands." His very seat of dwelling is in their hearts. The Bible uses the term *naos.* That is a word used by the ancient Greeks to refer to the very niche in a pagan temple where the idol or image of the temple god or goddess was placed. Paul tells us that our hearts, by God's grace, have become the very niche where the true God dwells.

This behooves us to purify God's *naos,* His niche within, to cleanse and rededicate our whole being to His service.

Will you dedicate, again this day, your heart and your life to the service of God, both in this sanctuary and the great chapel of God that is the world?

Congregation: We will and do so dedicate ourselves.

PRAYER FOR THE DEDICATION OF THE PEOPLE OF GOD

Here the district superintendent, or the pastor, may
lead the litany.

Let us signify our dedication to God as a
called-out community of faith by praying together.

Congregation: Almighty God, to whom all
hearts are open,
all desires known,
and from whom no secrets are hidden,
cleanse the thoughts of our hearts,
by the inspiration of Your Holy Spirit,
so that we may perfectly love You,
and worthily magnify Your holy name.
Through Jesus Christ our Lord. Amen.

CONGREGATIONAL SONG: "For Such a Time as
This"

CLOSING PRAYER

POSTLUDE

Rite Two

The following ritual is a more abbreviated rite of dedication, found in the *Manual of the Church of the Nazarene.*

Minister: Having been prospered by the hand of the Lord and enabled by His grace and strength to complete this building to the glory of His name, we now stand in God's presence to dedicate this structure to the service of His kingdom.

To the glory of God our Father, from whom cometh every good and perfect gift; to the honor of Jesus Christ, our Lord and Savior; and to the praise of the Holy Spirit, Source of light, and life, and power—our Sanctifier,

Congregation: We do now, with joy and gratitude, humbly dedicate this building.

Minister: In remembrance of all who have loved and served this church, establishing the heritage we now enjoy, and who are now part of the Church Triumphant,

Congregation: We gratefully dedicate this edifice (sanctuary, education building, fellowship hall, etc.).

Minister: For worship in prayer and song, for the preaching of the Word, for the teaching of the Scriptures, and for the fellowship of the saints,

Congregation: We solemnly dedicate this house of God.

Minister: For the comfort of those who mourn, for the strengthening of the weak, for the help of those who are tempted, and for the giving of hope and courage to all who come within these walls,

Congregation: We dedicate this place of fellowship and prayer.

Minister: For the sharing of the good news of salvation from sin, for the spreading of scriptural holiness, for the giving of instruction in righteousness, and for the service of our fellowmen,

Congregation: We reverently dedicate this building.

Unison: We, as laborers together with God, now join hands and hearts and dedicate ourselves anew to the high and holy purposes to which this building has been set apart. We pledge our loyal devotion, faithful stewardship, and diligent service to the end that in this place the name of the Lord shall be glorified, and His kingdom shall be advanced; through Jesus Christ our Lord. Amen.

Litany for Closing a Sanctuary[7]

This litany is intended for use when a new sanctuary is being prepared and the congregation wishes to give acknowledgment and gratitude for the previous place of worship that has served their needs and been the site from which they have moved in service to Christ and the world around.

Minister: Let us give thanks to Almighty God for mercies bestowed here in past years.

For the erection and dedication of this house to Your honor and glory as a place of worship, reaching, and service, and for the witness in faith and life that has here been given to the people of these generations,

People: We thank You, Lord.

Minister: For all those servants of God who have led Your people in worship here, who have preached Your Word from this pulpit, and who have administered the sacraments to waiting and believing hearts,

People: We thank You, Lord.

Minister: For sacred song and music, for drama and story and ceremony that have helped people see the objectives and directions of Christian living,

People: We thank You, Lord.

Minister: For all those who have come to this

place seeking You, and who, in worshiping You in spirit and in truth, have found You,

People: We thank You, Lord.

Minister: For those who have brought their children here for Christian baptism or dedication, for those who have pledged their love to one another at Your holy altar, and for those who in Christian faith and trust have here parted with a loved one and committed that loved one to Your love and care,

People: We thank You, Lord.

Minister: For sins that have been confessed and forgiven here, for burdens that have been made easier to carry, for distressed and troubled hearts that have known the peace that passes all understanding, and for lives that have been inspired to new heights of love and service, for hearts that have been cleansed, and lives that have been possessed of the love of God and humankind,

People: We thank You, Lord.

Minister: For all this building has meant to congregation, visitor, and town; for the walls of security, the overarching of love, the support of encouragement, the halls of friendship, the lessons of humanity, the lights of faith, and the doorways to service,

People: We thank You, Lord.

Minister: Bless us, we pray, as we go from here; and, as our new church home grows about us, may we be bound together in the glorious adventure of building for You a house of life and heart and service, to the glory of Your name and the extending of Your kingdom, in the name of the Creator and of the Son and of the Holy Spirit.

Unison: Now unto Him who is able to keep us from falling, and to present us faultless before the presence of His glory with exceeding joy, to the only wise God, our Savior, be glory and majesty, dominion and power, both now and forever.

Minister: The grace of our Lord Jesus Christ, the love of God, and the communion of the Holy Spirit be with you evermore. Amen.

The minister hands the pulpit Bible to the secretary of the congregation, and the official board escorts it from the sanctuary. The Bible represents the people's place of worship, and this action shows that the place of worship will be in the care of the official board until the dedication of a new building, at which time it will be placed on the pulpit of the new church home.

Ritual for the Dedication of a Parsonage[8]

Minister: In the name of God, the Creator, and of the Son and of the Holy Spirit. Amen.

People: We have assembled here to dedicate this house unto God.

Trustee: As those to whom the responsibility of maintaining this house has been committed, we now express our willingness to dedicate it unto Him who is the Master Builder and the Keeper of all, whose we are and whom we serve.

Minister: To what ends and for what purposes do you wish to dedicate this house?

Unison: As a fitting and pleasant place where our pastor and family can make their home.

As a place where study and meditation on the Holy Scripture may be pursued.

As a place where Christian fellowship may be had, where we have shared both our joys and our sorrows, our successes and our shortcomings, and strengthen the ties that bind our hearts in Christian love.

As a place where the confidential counsel of God's ministering servant can be found.

And as a quiet and comfortable place of refuge and relief to which God's servant can return when at times the duties and responsibilities of the office bear heavily.

To these ends and for the glory of God, we now dedicate this parsonage.

Minister: O God, You have heard the expressed desires of these Your people for whose spiritual well-being I am responsible. Accept, we ask You, this house that they with their gifts and their labor do provide and shall endeavor to maintain.

Grant indeed, gracious God, that we may all do our part to keep it always for the high purposes to which they have now pledged it. And may all who shall ever dwell herein live lives that bear steadfast witness to the Savior, that Your blessed and holy benediction may rest upon it now and as long as it shall stand.

In the name of Jesus Christ, our Lord. Amen.

Unison:
> *Bless this house, O Lord, we pray,*
> *Make it safe by night and day;*
> *Bless these walls, so firm and stout,*
> *Keeping want and trouble out;*
> *Bless the roof and chimneys tall,*
> *Let Thy peace lie over all;*
> *Bless this door, that it may prove*
> *Ever open to joy and love.*
> *Bless these windows shining bright,*
> *Letting in God's heavenly light;*
> *Bless the hearth ablazing there,*
> *With smoke ascending like a prayer;*
> *Bless the folk who dwell within,*

Keep them pure and free from sin;
Bless us all that we may be
Fit, O Lord, to dwell with Thee,
Bless us all that one day we
May dwell, O Lord, with Thee. Amen.†
                              —Helen Taylor

Ritual for the Dedication of a Home†

DEDICATION OF A HOME

Minister: Peace be to this house,

People: And to all who dwell therein.

Minister: Our help is in the name of the Lord,

People: Who made heaven and earth.

Minister: Peace be within your walls,

People: And prosperity within your palaces.

Minister: For my brothers', sisters', and friends' sakes, I will now say:

People: Peace be with you. Glory be to the Father and to the Son and to the Holy Ghost. As it was in the beginning, is now, and ever shall be, world without end. Amen.

SCRIPTURE: *Prov. 24:3-4*

Minister: Let us pray. O Lord God, Your gifts are many, and in wisdom You have made all things to give You glory. We ask You to bless those who live in this place. Visit with Your love and gladness all who come and go, and preserve us all in peace, through Jesus Christ our Lord. Amen.

A CANDLE IS LIGHTED

SCRIPTURE: *Matt. 5:14-16*

Minister: Let us pray. O God, as this candle gives light to this home, so enable those who dwell here to be Your light in the world, through Jesus Christ our Lord. Amen.

SCRIPTURE: *Matt. 7:24-27*

Minister: Let us pray. O God, from whom the whole family in heaven and earth is named, be present in this home, that all who live here, having genuine affection for one another, may find here a haven of blessing and of peace, through Jesus Christ our Lord. Amen.

SCRIPTURE: *Luke 19:1-10*

Minister: Let us pray. O God, refresh all who visit here, that they may know friendship and love, through Jesus Christ our Lord. Amen.

SCRIPTURE: *Ps. 121:8*

Minister: Let us pray. O God, protect and guide those who live here, their going out and their coming in; and let them share the hospitality of this home with all who visit, that those who enter here may know Your love and peace, through Jesus Christ our Lord. Amen.

SCRIPTURE: *John 13:34-35*

Minister: Let us pray. O God, be present with those who come here for fellowship and recreation, that thcy may be renewed and refreshed, through Jesus Christ our Lord. Amen.

SCRIPTURE: *Acts 2:46-47*

Minister: Let us pray. To live with You, O Lord, is to be at home with ourselves. Now be with us, we pray, as we dedicate this place as a home for _____. Bless these personal things of taste and choice that put the mark of these particular people upon it and make it theirs. May it be a place of shelter and protection, of rest and healing, of warmth and hospitality. And may Your embracing love be seen and felt in all the celebrations, daily chores, hard decisions, and shared glories that will occur here. As it will become the storehouse of blessed memories, make it also a place for growth in grace. We pray in the name of Him who has prepared a place for us, in whose house are many rooms, even Jesus Christ our Lord. Amen.

LORD'S PRAYER

Minister: The Lord watch over our going out and our coming in from this time forth forever. Amen.

DOXOLOGY

Other Rituals

OTHER RITUALS

Seasonal Services
Advent

The following services are designed to guide a church in the celebration of Advent, which is the beginning of the Christian year. The season of Advent begins with the fourth Sunday before Christmas, which is the Sunday nearest November 30, and continues to Christmas Eve. The word "Advent" derives from the Latin *adventus,* which means "coming." The season proclaims the comings of Christ—whose birth we prepare to celebrate once again, who comes continually in Word and Spirit, and whose return in final victory we anticipate. Therefore, Advent looks both backward to Jesus' first coming at Bethlehem and forward to His coming again at the end.

We begin the Christian year by reflecting on the end of history. The message of many of the Advent hymns have a note of threat and promise in contrast to the more traditional Christmas carols. This emphasis points to the thrust of the readings and sermons most usually associated with Advent. Those churches that utilize the Revised Common Lectionary, or other ordered readings in conjunction with the observance of the Christian year, find that the readings for Advent deal not so much with preparation for Christmas as with the expectation of Christ's return in glory to rule, judge, and save. The prayer of this season is expressed in the phrases of the Lord's Prayer: "Thy kingdom come, thy will be done, on earth" (Matt. 6:10, RSV). There is a strong prophetic note in this season announcing judgment upon evil, combined with an emphasis on hope and the expectation of Christ's coming reign in glory.

Various colors and combinations of colors are suggested for use during Advent and Christmas. Purple or blue banners and paramounts are suggested for Advent, while white,

yellow, and gold are suggested for the celebration of Christmas Eve and Day.

The Advent wreath, often used in churches and in homes,
is an evergreen wreath with four purple candles and a central white Christ candle added or lighted on Christmas Eve
or Christmas Day.

The Hanging of the Greens[9]

Some churches celebrate the beginning of Advent with a service of the Hanging of the Greens. Other churches observe the
service at other times during Advent. The service may be used
on a Sunday morning during the opening of the service or as a
response to the Word. It may also be used as an evening service.
During the singing of "Come, Thou Long-expected Jesus,"
greens may be brought in and the Advent candle lighted.

In the service of the Hanging of the Greens, each of the
lessons should, if possible, be read by a different reader.
Each reader should announce the lesson by the descriptive
title preceding it. At the end of the lesson, the reader or another person reads the narrative.

INTRODUCTION*

Reader 1: How shall we prepare this house for
the coming of the King?

Reader 2: With branches of cedar, the tree of
royalty.

Reader 1: How shall we prepare this house for
the coming of the eternal Christ?

Reader 2: With garlands of pine and fir, whose
leaves are ever living, ever green.

Reader 1: How shall we prepare this house for
the coming of our Savior?

Reader 2: With wreaths of holly and ivy, telling of His passion, death, and resurrection.

Reader 1: How shall we prepare our hearts for the coming of the Son of God?

Reader 2: By hearing again the words of the prophets, who foretold the saving work of God.

Reader 1: For God did not send the Son into the world to condemn the world, but that the world through him might be saved.

Reader 2: Glory to God in the highest!

GOD WILL SEND A RIGHTEOUS KING (Jer. 23:5-6)

Reader 3: In ancient times the cedar was revered as the tree of royalty.

It also signified immortality and was used for purification.

We place this cedar branch as a sign of Christ, who reigns as King forever, and whose coming, in justice and righteousness, will purify our hearts.

HYMN

Suggested hymns: "Come, Thou Long-expected Jesus," *Sing to the Lord* (STTL), 157; "Jesus Shall Reign," STTL, 271; "Rejoice, the Lord Is King," STTL, 276

THE PROPHET DECLARES A CHILD WILL BE BORN (Isa. 9:2, 6-7)

Because the needles of pine and fir trees appear

not to die each season, the ancients saw them as signs of things that last forever. Isaiah tells us that there will be no end to the reign of the Messiah. Therefore, we hand this wreath of evergreens shaped in a circle, which itself has no end, to signify the eternal reign of Jesus, the Christ.

HYMN

> Suggested hymn: "O Come, O Come, Emmanuel," STTL, 163

THE FOURTH SERVANT SONG (Isa. 53:1-6)

For Christians, passage from Isaiah reflects the sufferings of Jesus, who saved us from our sins by His death on the Cross and by His resurrection from the dead.

In ancient times, holly and ivy were considered signs of Christ's passion. Their prickly leaves suggested the crown of thorns, the red berries the blood of the Savior, and the bitter bark the drink offered to Jesus on the Cross.

As we hang the holly and the ivy, let us rejoice in the coming of Jesus, our Savior.

HYMN

> Suggested hymns: "I Lay My Sins on Jesus," STTL, 340; "I Know a Fount," STTL, 252

THE MYSTERY OF THE INCARNATION* (John 1:1-5, 9-14)

As we prepare for the coming of Jesus, the

Light of the World, we light the Christmas tree.
During this Advent, wherever you see a lighted
Christmas tree, let it call to mind the One who
brings light to our darkness, healing to our bro-
kenness, and peace to all who receive Him.

The tree is now lighted.

HYMN

Suggested hymn: "Emmanuel," STTL, 165

THE BLESSING OF THE TREE

Many churches allow children to participate in bringing
decorations for the tree. In some cases, use of a Christmas tree encourages those who decorate the tree to use
symbolic decorations that depict some dimension of the
life and ministry of Christ, such as stars, fish, or other
symbols. A blessing is pronounced for the tree and its
meaning, often preceded by the reading of Titus 3:4-7. In
some churches, the tree trunk is saved to make a cross
for Lent. The following blessing is suggested for use:

Holy Lord,

we come with joy to celebrate the birth of Your Son,
who rescued us from the darkness of sin
by making the Cross a tree of life and light.

May this tree, arrayed in splendor,
remind us of the life-giving cross of Christ,
that we may always rejoice
in the new life that shines on our hearts.

We ask this through Christ our Lord.

Amen.[10]

Blessings of the Advent Wreath

The Advent wreath is a simple circle of evergreen branches, a sign of life without end; its four Advent candles encircle a central white Christ candle. Some traditions use the color rose on the third Sunday of Advent and for this reason use three purple candles and one rose candle. The following blessing, with a reading from Isa. 9:2, 6-7, may precede the lighting of the first Advent candle. This blessing may also be used for blessing an Advent wreath in a home.

Reader 1: Christ came to bring us salvation and has promised to come again.

Let us pray that we may always be ready to welcome Him.

Reader 2: Come, Lord Jesus.

Reader 1: Let us pray that the keeping of Advent may open our hearts to God's love.

Reader 2: Come, Lord Jesus.

Reader 1: Let us pray that the light of Christ may penetrate the darkness of sin.

Reader 2: Come, Lord Jesus.

Reader 1: Let us pray that this wreath may constantly remind us to prepare for the coming of Christ.

Reader 2: Come, Lord Jesus.

Reader 1: Let us pray that the Christmas season may fill us with peace and joy as we strive to follow the example of Jesus.

Reader 2: Come, Lord Jesus.

Reader 1: Loving God, Your Church joyfully awaits the coming of its Savior, who enlightens our hearts and dispels the darkness of ignorance and sin.

Pour forth Your blessings upon us as we light the candles of this wreath.

May their light reflect the splendor of Christ, who is Lord, for ever and ever. Amen.[11]

LIGHTING OF THE ADVENT CANDLES

Each Sunday of Advent may include the lighting of the Advent candles by an appointed family or person. This is usually done early in the service. Each Sunday one additional candle is lighted until all four are lighted. Finally, on Christmas Eve and Day, the middle white candle is lighted. The person lighting the candles, or another assisting them, may say the words provided for each Sunday. The candles may be lighted during or after the reading of the Scripture lessons or while a hymn is sung or other appropriate words are spoken.

Suggested Readings:

FIRST SUNDAY—Isa. 60:2-3

We light this candle as a symbol of Christ our Hope.

May the light sent from God shine in the darkness to show us the way of salvation.

O come, O come, Emmanuel.

SECOND SUNDAY—Mark 1:4

We light this candle as a symbol of Christ the Way.

May the Word sent from God through the prophets lead us to the way of salvation.

O come, O come, Emmanuel.

THIRD SUNDAY—Isa. 35:10

We light this candle as a symbol of Christ our Joy.

May the joyful promise of Your presence, O God, make us rejoice in our hope of salvation.

O come, O come, Emmanuel.

FOURTH SUNDAY—Isa. 9:6-7

We light this candle as a symbol of the Prince of Peace.

May the visitation of Your Holy Spirit, O God, make us ready for the coming of Jesus, our Hope and Joy.

O come, O come, Emmanuel.[12]

Creative Worship Bulletin Ideas
for Christmas[13]

First Sunday of Advent

There's a Song in the Air
We are greeted in the name of the Lord Jesus.
The pastor shares.
We prepare our hearts for worship.

There's a Star in the Sky
The choir calls us to worship.
The lighting of the Advent wreath.
+Congregational hymn.
Congregational hymn.*

There's a Tumult of Joy
A moment for friendship.
We worship with His tithes and our offerings.
Congregational hymn.
We come into His presence.
Bring your needs to the altar.
Scripture reading.

We Rejoice in the Light
The sanctuary choir.
Silent prayer for our pastor.
Today's good news by the pastor.

Second Sunday of Advent

Come, Thou Long-expected Jesus
God's forever family gathers.
Share a moment with the pastor.
Quietly ask God's blessing upon the service.
Meditate upon Luke 2.

Born to Set Thy People Free
The choir calls us to worship.
We celebrate Advent as we sing a hymn.*
The lighting of the Advent wreath.
Congregational hymn.

Israel's Strength and Consolation
It is family altar time.
The choir calls us to prayer.
We bring our praise and petitions to the altar.
The choir ministers to us.
A moment for friendship.
We worship with His tithes and our offerings.
Special music.

Joy of Every Longing Heart
Today's good news by the pastor.
Closing hymn.*

Third Sunday of Advent

Hark! the Herald Angels Sing
The pastor greets us.
We prepare our hearts for worship.

Glory to the Newborn King!
The choir calls us to worship.
The lighting of the Advent wreath.
+Congregational hymn.
Congregational hymn.*

Veiled in Flesh the Godhead See
A moment for friendship.
We worship with His tithes and our offerings.
Congregational hymn.
We come into His presence.
Bring your needs to the altar.
Scripture reading.

Hail th'incarnate Deity!
The sanctuary choir.
Silent prayer for our pastor.
Today's good news by the pastor.

Fourth Sunday of Advent

O Come, All Ye Faithful
A Christmas greeting.
A moment for reflection.

Yea, Lord, We Greet Thee
The choir leads us in praise and adoration.
We share in the Christmas event by singing a
hymn.*
The lighting of the Advent wreath.

Come and Behold Him
The choir calls us to prayer.
The Christmas altar is open.
We bring to King Jesus our gifts.
We ask for help with our needs.
Sanctuary choir.
We present to our Lord His tithes and our offerings.
A moment for friendship.

Word of the Father
Special music.
Today's good news by the pastor.
Closing hymn.*

A Service of Carols and Candles

ORGAN PRELUDE

THE PROCESSIONAL CHRISTMAS CAROL

The congregation will rise as the choir enters.

"O Come, All Ye Faithful" (Adeste Fidelis, trans. Frederick Oakeley et al.)

THE CALL TO WORSHIP

Minister: "In the beginning was the Word."

People: "And the Word was with God, and the Word was God."

Minister: "All things were made by him."

People: "And without him was not any thing made that was made."

Minister: "In him was life."

People: "And the life was the light of men."

Unison: Let our light so shine before men, that they may see our good works, and glorify our Father in heaven. Amen!

The congregation will be seated.

The Light Revealed

A PROPHECY
Isa. 9:6-7; Luke 1:26-33

A CHRISTMAS CAROL

Congregation and choir

"O Little Town of Bethlehem" (Phillips Brooks)

The Light Received

A CHRISTMAS SCRIPTURE READING—Luke 2:1-18

A CHRISTMAS CAROL

Congregation and choir

"It Came upon the Midnight Clear" (Edmund H. Sears)

THE CHRISTMAS OFFERING

A CHRISTMAS ANTHEM

The choir

THE CHRISTMAS PRAYER

A CHRISTMAS MEDITATION

A CHRISTMAS CAROL

Congregation and choir

"Hark! the Herald Angels Sing" (Charles Wesley)

The Light Reflected
(A Service of Lights)

THE DISTRIBUTION OF CANDLES

The pastor will light his candle; the ushers will light their candles from the pastor's candle; the ushers will then move down the aisle, lighting the candles of the congregation in this manner: The worshipers nearest the center aisle will receive the light and in turn give their light to the one by their side. "Silent Night!" should be sung softly and reverently, with no other light burning but the candles. The candles should not be extinguished until the close of the Lord's Prayer.

A Christmas Carol
Congregation standing

"Silent Night!" (Joseph Mohr, trans. John F. Young)

The Closing Prayer of Dedication
Followed by the Lord's Prayer

Benediction

The Recessional Christmas Carol
Congregation and choir

"Joy to the World" (Isaac Watts, Antioch)

Organ Postlude

Christmas Sunday

Welcome and Merry Christmas! It is Christmas Sunday, and what joy it is to celebrate the birth of our Lord and Savior Jesus Christ, in His house, with His people. Today we celebrate not only His original coming but His coming into our hearts individually and the promise of His return to unite us with Him forever. Our joining with the sights and sounds of the Advent season is now complete. Come, let us worship our King!

Organ Prelude

We Are Called to Celebrate
Through music: "He Is Born"
Sanctuary choir and balcony brass

Through the reading of Scripture: Luke 2:21-35
Through our Advent liturgy

See below

WE CELEBRATE IN SONG
"Joy to the World" (Isaac Watts)
"I Heard the Bells on Christmas Day" (Henry W. Longfellow)
"O Come, All Ye Faithful" (trans. Frederick Oakeley et al.)

WE JOIN OUR HEARTS AND MINDS IN PRAYER
Refrain: "O Come, Let Us Adore Him"
Pastoral prayer
"Simeon took him in his arms and praised God" (Luke 2:28, NIV). We would do as Simeon did.

OUR WORSHIP CELEBRATION CONTINUES
Through music: "Simeon's Song"

Sanctuary choir and balcony brass

As we fellowship
As we give

Offertory

WE ARE MINISTERED TO
In song: "Let This Child Be Born in You"

Sanctuary choir and balcony brass

By message from the Word: "Simeon Saw Salvation in a Baby"

WE RESPOND

OUR PRAYER OF BENEDICTION

We depart "praising God, and saying, Glory to God in the highest, and on earth peace, good will toward men" (Luke 2:13-14).

COME SHARE THE JOY!

ADVENT CANDLE LITURGY

First Reader: Today is the fourth and last Sunday of Advent. We return again to the festive wreath with the question, "What do you see?"

Second Reader: The first candle represents Zechariah, who saw an angel but also saw reconciliation between God and man.

First Reader: The second candle stands for the magi, who saw a star and recognized sovereignty.

Second Reader: The third candle stands for the shepherds, who saw a Savior in a manger.

First Reader: This fourth candle represents Simeon, whose eyes longed to see "the consolation of Israel."

Second Reader: He saw a baby in His mother's arms. But he saw more. He saw "the Lord's Christ"! And he rejoiced.

First Reader: We also see the Lord's Christ in Jesus.

Second Reader: And we rejoice!

Easter[14]

The Tenebrae Service
The Vigil of Darkness
A Service of Lights

PRELUDE
  "There Is a Fountain"

  Handbell choir

INTRODUCTION TO THE TENEBRAE SERVICE

INVOCATION

Minister: Let us pray. O God, this is a night filled with memory and hope. Let us remember.

People: And so we remember that we are made of clay, molded in Your image.

Minister: We think about yesterday and sigh; and we are anxious about tomorrow.

People: May Your presence fill the room and remove the guilt of yesterday and give us purpose for tomorrow. Remind us again that we are accepted.

Minister: Make our acceptance of ourselves and each other complete through Christ our Lord. Amen.

FIRST LIGHT

The Darkness of Betrayal
  Hymn: "O Jesus, I Have Promised"

SECOND LIGHT

The Darkness of Desertion
  Hymn: "O Love That Will Not Let Me Go"

THIRD LIGHT

The Darkness of Disunity
  Hymn: "'Tis Midnight"

FOURTH LIGHT

The Darkness of Disloyalty
  Hymn: "Must Jesus Bear the Cross Alone?"

FIFTH LIGHT

The Darkness of Denial
  Chancel choir: "Beneath the Cross of Jesus"

SIXTH LIGHT

The Darkness of the Cross
  Chancel choir: "O Sacred Head, Now Wounded"

THE SACRAMENT OF HOLY COMMUNION

TRIO

  "Precious Blood"

SEVENTH LIGHT

The Darkness of Light
  Hymn: "On the Cross of Calvary"

BENEDICTION

Minister: "For, behold, the darkness shall cover the earth, and gross darkness the people."

People: "But the LORD shall arise upon thee, and his glory shall be seen upon thee."

Minister: "And the Gentiles shall come to thy light, and kings to the brightness of thy rising."

People: Lord, Thou hast broken bread with us in fellowship, and Thy broken body reminds us of our death. Break this fellowship and scatter us out upon Thy world, and by Thy grace bring us together again at Thy table, through Him who is the Light of the World, even Jesus Christ, our Lord. Amen.

POSTLUDE

—Courtesy of Robert Simmons

Tenebrae Service
by Virginia Cameron

Two varied examples of a Tenebrae service outline are provided here for your referral. Note that instructions and a brief explanation as to the history and nature of the service are included in the bulletin or worship folder for each worshiper.

The beauty of this service is its simplicity and its adaptability to any size of congregation, and it can be tailored to local church tastes and worship styles, depending on the music selected for each segment.

Service One
Tenebrae
A Service of Darkness

ORGAN PRELUDE

SCRIPTURE MEDITATION
"For, behold, the darkness shall cover the earth, and gross darkness the people: but the LORD shall arise upon thee, and his glory shall be seen upon thee" (Isa. 60:2).

"And the light shineth in darkness; and the darkness comprehended it not" (John 1:5).

THE LAST SUPPER
Hymn: "According to Thy Gracious Word"
Scripture
The Last Supper

Pastoral meditation

Hymn: "Here at Thy Table, Lord"

Communion

GETHSEMANE
   Scripture
   Hymn: "'Tis Midnight"

THE DENIAL AND TRIAL
   Scripture
   Hymn: "Lead Me to Calvary" (vv. 1 and 4)

THE SUFFERING SERVANT
   Responsive Reading
   Hymn: "Just as I Am"

CHRIST SENTENCED
   Scripture
   Hymn: "O Sacred Head, Now Wounded"

ON THE WAY TO THE CROSS
   Scripture
   Duet: "Blessed Redeemer"

CRUCIFIXION
   Scripture
   Silent Prayer
   Organ Meditation: "There Is a Fountain"

DISMISSAL
   Please reverently preserve this hour of remembrance, and leave the church building in silence.
   Ponder these things in your heart.
   "And there was a darkness over all the earth . . . And the sun was darkened" (Luke 23:44-45).

Service Two
Tenebrae
A Service of Shadows

ORGAN PRELUDE AND SILENT PRAYERS

CHORAL MEDITATION
  "O Come and Mourn with Me Awhile"

CONGREGATIONAL HYMN
  "There Is a Green Hill Far Away"

PRAYER
  The Lord's Prayer

SHADOWS OF HOLY WEEK

1. The Shadow of His Body Broken for Us
   Scripture: Matt. 26:26-29
   Hymn: "Bread of the World in Mercy Broken"
   The Eucharist
   Prayer of Thanksgiving

2. The Shadow of the Betrayal
   Scripture: Matt. 26:17-25
   Ensemble: "Ah, Holy Jesus"

3. The Servant
   Responsive Reading
   Hymn: "O Sacred Head, Now Wounded"
   Scripture: John 13:1-17

4. The Shadow of the Desertion
   Scripture: Matt. 26:31-35
   Hymn: "'Tis Midnight"

5. The Shadow of an Unshared Vigil

Scripture: Matt. 26:36-45
Hymn: "'Tis Midnight"

6. The Arrest at the Gate
Scripture: John 18:1-5
Ensemble: "Go to Dark Gethsemane"

7. The Shadow of the Cross
Scripture: Mark 15:16-20
Songs of the Cross
Congregational medley

DARKNESS
Silence

THE RETURN OF THE LIGHT

BENEDICTION

DISMISSAL

Please leave the church in silence, allowing your heart to ponder these things.

A Word About This Service

The ancient Tenebrae service dates back to the early centuries of the Christian Church. Coming from the Latin word meaning "shadows," Tenebrae depicts the flight of the disciples and the approaching Crucifixion. It summarizes the events and teachings that occurred in Holy Week from Maundy Thursday and Good Friday, preparatory to the Resurrection on Easter Sunday.

As you enter, meditate that it was Maundy Thursday when the 12 disciples were with Jesus in the Upper Room for the last time, and that He and they stood in the shadow of the Cross.

The extinguishing of the candles and lights as the service progresses symbolizes the approaching hour of the Crucifixion. The time of total darkness recalls the hours Christ was in the tomb. The return of the light is prophetic of the Easter soon to dawn.

Think and pray on the meaning this service has for you and for the church.

Maundy Thursday Service

With Christ . . .
  At the feet of Peter
  At the Passover meal
  In the Garden of Gethsemane

SCRIPTURE FOR THE EVENING: John 13:1-17; Matt. 26:26-30; Matt. 26:36-50

WORSHIP LEADERS

ORDER OF SERVICE

ORGAN PRELUDE
  "O Sacred Head, Now Wounded" (tune: Hassler, arranged by Bach)

GREETING AND CALL TO WORSHIP
  Hymn: "There Is a Green Hill Far Away"

WITH CHRIST AT THE FEET OF PETER
  Scripture reading: John 13:1-17
  The meaning of "maundy"
  A prayer of application
  "Must Jesus Bear the Cross Alone?"

WITH CHRIST AT THE PASSOVER MEAL
  Scripture reading: Matt. 26:26-30
  The Passover meal and the Lord's Supper
  Holy Communion
  "Were You There?"

WITH CHRIST IN THE GARDEN OF GETHSEMANE
Scripture reading: Matt. 26:36-50
"'Tis Midnight"
Lest We Forget Gethsemane
Hymn: "Lead Me to Calvary"

BENEDICTION

ORGAN POSTLUDE
"Lift High the Cross"
"Let us go quietly . . ."

Pastor: O Lord, You who came to call sinners to repentance:

People: Call us still that we may answer.

Pastor: You who did meet the hardness of the thief:

People: Soften the hearts of all who are impenitent.

Pastor: You who did call Zacchaeus from the sycamore tree:

People: Arouse the careless and arrest the curious.

Pastor: You who did speak words of spirit and of life:

People: Enlighten the ignorant and teach the unlearned.

Pastor: Dispel all prejudice and correct all error:

People: Establish Your people in the truth of Your gospel.

Pastor: You who did pray for Your murderers:

People: Pity those who persecute Your servants.

Pastor: You who did call out many devils:

People: Set free by the power of Your grace the many who are victims of pride and anger, of greed and selfishness.

Pastor: You who did satisfy the doubts of Thomas:

People: Deal gently with those who can scarcely believe.

Pastor: You who did uplift the sinking Peter:

People: Support all who are weak and unstable.

Pastor: You who did proclaim deliverance to the captives:

People: Pity all prisoners and loose the bonds of their sin.

Pastor: You who did raise the dead to life:

People: Quicken us all to life in Your righteousness.

Pastor: You who did come to save Your people from their sins:

People: Save, O Lord, those who put their trust in You.

Easter Sunday

Welcome to the grandest day of celebration of the Church year—Easter Sunday! It is without a doubt a glorious day for us to gather to worship our risen Lord—the King of Kings and Lord of Lords, the Great High Priest of the Kingdom of Light. Come now into His presence in a spirit of jubilant celebration, proclaiming that He is risen indeed!

ORGAN PRELUDE

WE ARE CALLED TO CELEBRATE
In an Easter call to worship

CHOIR AND INSTRUMENTATION
"Christ Is Risen: Alleluia!"

WE CELEBRATE IN SONG
Hymn: "Christ, the Lord, Is Risen Today"

Youth handbells

Hymn: "Christ Arose"
Hymn: "Hallelujah! What a Savior!"

WE JOIN IN PRAYER
Pastoral prayer

Pastor

Welcome to God by the new and *living Way!*

OUR CELEBRATION CONTINUES
Through music: "All Glory, Laud, and Honor"

Youth handbells

As we fellowship

Pastor

As we give

Offertory

WE ARE MINISTERED TO

In song: "Great Is Jehovah the Lord" (from *How Great Thou Art,* written by Franz Schubert, arranged by David T. Clydesdale; sanctuary choir and instrumentation)

Through His servant: "The Light Breaks Forth—Victorious"

Pastor

WE RESPOND

In a prayer of benediction

Pastor

WE DEPART

Continuing to celebrate and worship the risen Christ

Lord's Day Morning

Let an atmosphere of worship begin with the organ prelude. Use these moments to enter privately into a spirit of prayer and praise.

ORGAN PRELUDE

CHORAL CALL TO WORSHIP
"Rejoice, the Lord Is King" (arranged by Fettke)

INVOCATION

CONGREGATIONAL HYMNS
"Christ, the Lord, Is Risen Today"
"Christ Arose"

SCRIPTURE READING
Matt. 28:1-7

PRAYER TIME

CHORAL CALL TO PRAYER
"Easter Prayer" (arranged by Fettke)

PASTORAL PRAYER
Congregational response: "Alleluia"

CHANCEL CHOIR AND BRASS
"Easter Fanfare" (by Jane Marshall)

FRIENDSHIP TIME
Pass the friendship register.

ANNOUNCEMENTS

WORSHIP THROUGH GIVING
   Organ offertory

VOCAL SOLO

MORNING MESSAGE
   "The Easter Imperatives" (Matt. 28:1-7)

CLOSING

BENEDICTION

CHORAL BENEDICTION
   "An Easter Benediction" (by Edwin M. Willmington)

ORGAN POSTLUDE

And Can It Be?
A Celebration of the Atonement
Palm Sunday Evening

ORGAN PRELUDE
"Carillon de Westminster" (Louis Vierne)

CONGREGATIONAL HYMN
"Arise, My Soul, Arise"

WELCOME AND INVOCATION
"And Can It Be?" (Ovid Young, arranger)
"God So Loved the World" (John Stainer)
"God Hath Provided a Lamb" (Linda Almond; Ronn Huff, arranger)
"Hallelujah" (Mount of Olives; Beethoven)
"The Blood Will Never Lose Its Power" (Andrae Crouch; Dick Bolks, arranger)
"When I Survey the Wondrous Cross" (Ovid Young, arranger)

FRIENDSHIP/ANNOUNCEMENTS/OFFERING
Organ offertory: "Wondrous Love" (Dale Wood)
"Christ Arose" (Ronn Huff, arranger)
"Christ, Be Thine the Glory" (Heinrich Shutz)
"Because He Lives" (William Gaither; Ronn Huff, arranger)
"We Shall Behold Him" (Dottie Rambo; Ronn Huff, arranger)
"Hallelujah" (*Messiah,* G. F. Handel)

BENEDICTION

CHORAL BENEDICTION
  "The Lord Bless You and Keep You" (Lutkin)

ORGAN POSTLUDE
  "Fanfare" (Francis Jackson)

A Service of Healing

This service may be used in corporate worship, in the home or hospital room, in a prayer group meeting, or other appropriate setting. It is intended to express in both content and structure the confidence that God can and does heal, while it celebrates the reality that the ultimate hope of the Christian faith is not found in physical wellness but in the resurrection of the righteous.

GREETING AND PREPARATION

SCRIPTURE

Any one or more of the following scripture passages may serve as the foundation upon which a message may be built, or one or more of the passages may be read as scriptural warrant for the faith of the Church in God's attentiveness to the needs of His people.

2 Kings 5:1-19	Matt. 10:1-8
Ps. 13	Matt. 15:21-28
Ps. 23	Mark 5:24b-34
Ps. 27	Mark 10:46-52
Ps. 51:1-12, 15-17	Luke 5:17-26
Ps. 91	Luke 7:11-17
Ps. 103:1-5	Luke 17:11-19
Eccles. 3:1-11a	John 4:46-54
Isa. 35:1-10	John 5:2-18
Isa. 40:28-31	John 9
Isa. 43:1-3a, 18-19, 25	Acts 3:1-10
Isa. 53:3-5	Acts 5:12-16
Matt. 4:23-24	Rom. 8
Matt. 5:1-12	Rom. 14:7-12
Matt. 9:18-35	1 Cor. 12:4-11

2 Cor. 1:3-5   Heb. 12:1-2
2 Cor. 4:16-18   James 5:13-16
2 Cor. 12:7-10   1 John 5:13-15
Col. 1:11-29   Rev. 21:1-4

SERMON OR TESTIMONY

CONFESSION AND PARDON*

> If James 5:13-20, or portions thereof, has not been read
> earlier in the service, it may be read as a call to confes-
> sion to those whose hearts are hungry for redemption
> or for assurance and in preparation for anointing and
> prayer for healing.

> The minister may lead in a prayer of confession and
> supplication, inviting those present to respond in con-
> fession and faith.

> The Lord's Prayer

> A hymn of response and praise may be sung.

HOLY COMMUNION*

> The minister may administer Holy Communion to all
> present who wish to share in the Lord's table. The ser-
> vice may be adapted from the rituals suggested in this
> manual.

THANKSGIVING FOR THE OIL*

> The minister may pray an extemporaneous prayer or
> may pray the following prayer:

Let us pray:
O God, Giver of salvation and ultimate Source
of all healing, we give You thanks for the meaning of this symbol of Your presence. As Your disci-

ples were sent to heal the sick and anoint them in Your name, so we today follow the admonition of Your Word to anoint with oil this our brother (sister).

Pour out Your Holy Spirit on us, that those who in faith and repentance receive this anointing may be made whole; through Jesus Christ our Lord. Amen.

HYMN OF HEALING

The following suggested hymns or songs may be used: "Be Still and Know," "Come, Holy Spirit," "He Touched Me," "Rise and Be Healed," "There Is a Balm in Gilead."

PRAYERS FOR HEALING AND WHOLENESS WITH ANOINTING AND/OR LAYING ON OF HANDS

People may be invited to come forward individually or as a group to the altar or other prayer area. They may express any specific concerns or needs, and the minister or other designated persons may pray for them.

If there is anointing with oil, the minister or other leader shall touch a thumb or finger to the oil and touch the person's forehead with it, in silence, or using one of the following:

_____, I anoint you with oil in the name of the Father and of the Son and of the Holy Spirit _____ (for specific need).

May the power of the risen Christ be in you, and may His Holy Spirit heal you of all illnesses—of body, mind, spirit, and relationships—that you may serve God with a ready heart and a loving spirit. Amen.

Or,

_____, I lay my hands upon you and anoint you in the name of the Father and of the Son and of the Holy Spirit, beseeching our Lord Jesus Christ to sustain you with His presence, to drive away all sickness of body and spirit, and to give you that victory of life and peace that will enable you to serve Him both now and forevermore. Amen.

The minister may then add:

As you are outwardly anointed with this oil, so may our Heavenly Father grant you an inward anointing with the Holy Spirit.

May He release you from suffering and restore you to wholeness and strength.

May He deliver you from all evil, preserve you in all goodness, and bring you to everlasting life; through Jesus Christ our Lord. Amen.

PRAYER AFTER ANOINTING

The following, or another suitable prayer, may be used:

Almighty God, we pray that _____ (our brothers and sisters) may be comforted in their suffering and made whole. Grant them courage and strength, patience and hope.

May Your peace sustain them now and so preserve their hope that whenever death may come, they may be assured of Your welcome and may be received into Your open arms.

In the name of Jesus Christ our Lord. Amen.

TESTIMONIES OF PRAISE AND THANKSGIVING

Those who desire to do so may give thanks to God for healing or other blessings.

HYMN OF PRAISE

BENEDICTION AND DISMISSAL

An Order for Anointing and Prayer for Healing

The following may be used within a worship service or other setting where the desire has been expressed for anointing with oil and prayer for healing.

At an appropriate time in the service, those desiring anointing and prayer for healing may be invited to the altar with the following invitation:

We come to this moment with a certainty in God's care for all the life of His people. The Lord Jesus Christ, while He ministered on earth, was often about the work of healing physical infirmities as well as touching the deeper needs of people.

At this time of prayer today, I invite _____ to come forward for anointing, along with any others who desire the grace of anointing to be administered. We join in responding to the admonition of the Word as it is expressed for us in James 5:7-18. Those who wish to join _____ in support of his (her) petition in prayer, please come and kneel with him (her).

When the petitioner has come, along with any who desire to join with them, the minister may pray extempore or may use the following prayer:

O God, Giver of health and salvation: We cherish this oil as a symbol of Your presence with us, and as a reminder of Your interest in the whole of our existence spiritually, emotionally, and physically. As the holy apostles of Your Son, Jesus Christ, anointed many who were sick and healed them, so may those who in faith and repentance receive this holy unction be made whole; through Jesus Christ our Lord, who lives and reigns with You and with the Holy Spirit, one God, for ever and ever. Amen.

> The minister may then anoint those desiring it, touching the forehead of the petitioner with oil applied with the thumb or forefinger, and say:

I anoint you with oil in the name of the Father and of the Son and of the Holy Spirit, beseeching our Lord Jesus Christ to sustain you with His presence, to drive away all sickness of body and spirit, and to give you that victory of life and peace that will enable you to serve Him both now and evermore.

As you are outwardly anointed with this oil, so may the Father grant you the inward anointing of the Holy Spirit. May He forgive you your sins, release you from suffering, and restore you to wholeness and strength. May He deliver you from all evil, preserve you in all goodness, and bring you to everlasting life; through Jesus Christ our Lord. Amen.

A Service of Reconciliation

A service of reconciliation is intended for use in those cases when conflicts threaten to destroy the unity, harmony, and effectiveness of the Body of Christ. It should not be utilized for the minor or occasional differences that exist in churches or groups within the church that are the result of human frailty or differences caused by personality or preference.

The use of a Service of Reconciliation should be undertaken with the utmost caution and care. It should not be utilized too quickly, or with surface attempts to bridge over deep and underlying tensions that seriously divide people from one another, and which, unless resolved, may serve to do lasting harm to the offended parties, their families, and the witness of the Body of Christ.

This service is designed to culminate a series of intentional steps toward reconciliation. There should have been serious consultation with church leaders, fervent prayer, openness to the leadership of the Holy Spirit, careful searching of the Word for guidance, and an expressed desire on the part of all parties involved to seek reconciliation for the sake of the kingdom of God, the salvation of the lost, the sanctification of believers, and the effectiveness of the Church.

The leaders in the service should have consulted together and must have received the encouragement and participation of all parties in a dispute if a genuine reconciliation is to occur. The planning of the service should include participants in whatever conflict has threatened the fellowship. The service must be bathed in prayer, entered into with humility, and intended to bring to an end any enmity, strife, or ongoing alienation.

Suggested passages of scripture for background study include:

Gal. 5:1-26   Eph. 4:1—5:2   Phil. 4:2-9   Col. 3:1-17

The following service order is suggested for use:

GATHERING

Various hymns may be utilized for the gathering of the

people in preparation for the service. Among them are: "My Faith Looks Up to Thee," "Have Thine Own Way, Lord," "Jesus Paid It All," "Nearer, Still Nearer," "Our Great Savior."

WE ACKNOWLEDGE THE DESIRES OF GOD

Reader 1: One of the teachers of the law came and heard them debating. Noticing that Jesus had given them a good answer, he asked him, "Of all the commandments, which is the most important?"

"The most important one," answered Jesus, "is this: 'Hear, O Israel, the Lord our God, the Lord is one. Love the Lord your God with all your heart and with all your soul and with all your mind and with all your strength.' The second is this: 'Love your neighbor as yourself.' There is no commandment greater than these."

"Well said, teacher," the man replied. "You are right in saying that God is one and there is no other but him. To love him with all your heart, with all your understanding and with all your strength, and to love your neighbor as yourself is more important than all burnt offerings and sacrifices."

When Jesus saw that he had answered wisely, he said to him, "You are not far from the kingdom of God" (Mark 12:28-34, NIV).

Reader 2: For this is the message you have heard from the beginning, that we should love

one another. . . . We know that we have passed
from death to life because we love one another.
Whoever does not love abides in death. All who
hate a brother or sister are murderers, and you
know that murderers do not have eternal life
abiding in them. We know love by this, that he
laid down his life for us—and we ought to lay
down our lives for one another. . . . Little children, let us love, not in word or speech, but in
truth and action. . . . And this is his commandment, that we should believe in the name of his
Son Jesus Christ and love one another, just as he
has commanded us (1 John 3:11, 14-16, 18, 23,
NRSV).

Reader 3: "A new command I give you: Love
one another. As I have loved you, so you must
love one another. By this all men will know that
you are my disciples, if you love one another."

"As the Father has loved me, so have I loved
you. Now remain in my love. If you obey my commands, you will remain in my love, just as I have
obeyed my Father's commands and remain in his
love. I have told you this so that my joy may be in
you and that your joy may be complete. My command is this: Love each other as I have loved
you. Greater love has no one than this, that he
lay down his life for his friends. You are my
friends if you do what I command. . . . You did
not choose me, but I chose you and appointed you

to go and bear fruit—fruit that will last. Then the Father will give you whatever you ask in my name. This is my command: Love each other" (John 13:34-35; 15:9-14, 16-17, NIV).

WE ACKNOWLEDGE OUR NEED

Individually (Each participant in the service is asked to read the following in silence, standing, kneeling at the altar or at the pew, or seated.)

Have mercy on me, O God, according to your unfailing love; according to your great compassion blot out my transgressions. Wash away all my iniquity and cleanse me from my sin. For I know my transgressions, and my sin is always before me. Against you, you only, have I sinned and done what is evil in your sight, so that you are proved right when you speak and justified when you judge.

Surely you desire truth in the inner parts; you teach me wisdom in the inmost place. Cleanse me . . . and I will be clean; wash me, and I will be whiter than snow.

Create in me a pure heart, O God, and renew a steadfast spirit within me. . . . A broken and contrite heart, O God, you will not despise (Ps. 51:1-4, 6-7, 10, 17, NIV).

Corporately

Unison: Almighty and merciful God, we know that when we offend another, we offend You. We are aware that we have often allowed the shadow of hate to cloud our souls, hiding the light from our unseeing eyes. We have said unpleasant and hurtful things to our brothers and sisters when they have failed to live up to our expectations. Grant that we might find that spark of love that ever burns within us, the love that You have shown us even when we failed You. Fan the embers of that love until it roars again in flames of love, peace, and reconciliation. Forgive us our sins and help us to forgive those who have sinned against us. Lead us into new life through Your Son Jesus Christ, who died for the sins of all. Amen.[15]

WE PRAY THE LORD'S PRAYER

SCRIPTURE

"Therefore, as God's chosen people, holy and dearly loved, clothe yourselves with compassion, kindness, humility, gentleness and patience. Bear with each other and forgive whatever grievances you may have against one another. Forgive as the Lord forgave you. And over all these virtues put on love, which binds them all together in perfect unity.

Let the peace of Christ rule in your hearts, since as members of one body you were called to peace. And be thankful. Let the word of Christ dwelling in you richly as you teach and admonish one another with all wisdom, and as you sing psalms, hymns and spiritual songs with gratitude in your hearts to God. And whatever you do, whether in word or deed, do it all in the name of the Lord Jesus, giving thanks to God the Father through him" (Col. 3:12-17, NIV).

WE GRANT TO ONE ANOTHER THE PARDON OF CHRIST

Leader: It is the awesome privilege and responsibility of the Body of Christ to embody the grace of God. We therefore extend to others the grace He has extended to each of us. As Jesus commissioned His disciples to announce forgiveness to the contrite and repentant, so we announce His forgiveness to one another.

People: In the peace of Christ, and on the basis of His grace alone, I extend to you the forgiveness of Christ. I release you from guilt before me and stand with you all as brothers and sisters in Him.

Leader: Having granted forgiveness, we may with joy receive it. Let us embrace the pardon extended to us.

People: I receive your forgiveness as freely as Christ has provided it to us all. We stand forgiven in Him. I embrace the pardon you have given me and will live my life in gratitude to God and to you.

Leader: Let us commit ourselves to the pursuit of purity of heart and life before God and one another that is pleasing to Him.

People: May God himself, the God of peace, sanctify us through and through. May our spirits and souls and bodies be kept sound and blameless at the coming of our Lord Jesus Christ. The one who calls us is faithful, and He will do this.

WE CELEBRATE THE LORD'S SUPPER AS ONE

The administration of the Lord's Supper may be introduced by appropriate remarks or a brief homily and the reading of 1 Cor. 11:23-29; Luke 22:14-20; or some other suitable passage. Let the minister then give the following invitation:

The Lord himself ordained this holy sacrament. He commanded His disciples to partake of the bread and wine, emblems of His broken body and shed blood. This is His table. The feast is for His disciples. Let all those who have with true repentance forsaken their sins, and have believed in Christ unto salvation, draw near and take these emblems and, by faith, partake of the life of Jesus Christ, to your soul's comfort and joy. Let us remember that it is the memorial of the death and passion of our Lord; also a token of His coming again. Let us not forget that we are one, at one table with the Lord.

The minister may offer a prayer of confession and supplication, concluding with the following prayer of consecration:

Almighty God, who through Your tender mercy gave Your only Son, Jesus Christ, to suffer death upon the Cross for our redemption: hear us, we humbly pray. Grant that, as we receive these creatures of bread and wine according to the holy institution of Your Son, our Savior Jesus Christ, in remembrance of His passion and death, we may be made partakers of the benefits of His atoning sacrifice.

We are reminded that in the same night that our Lord was betrayed, He took bread and, when He had given thanks, He broke it and gave it to His disciples, saying, "Take, eat: this is My body, which is broken for you: do this in remembrance of Me." Likewise, after supper, He took the cup, and when He had given thanks, He gave it to them, saying, "Drink ye all of this, for this is My blood of the new testament, which is shed for you and for many, for the remission of sins; do this, as oft as ye shall drink it, in remembrance of Me."

May we come before You in true humility and faith as we partake of this holy sacrament. Through Jesus Christ our Lord. Amen.

Then may the minister, partaking first, with the assistance of any other ministers present and, when necessary, of the stewards, administer the Communion to the people.

While the bread is being distributed, let the minister say:

The body of our Lord Jesus Christ, which was broken for you, preserve you blameless unto everlasting life. Take and eat this, in remembrance that Christ died for you.

As the cup is being passed, let the minister say:

The blood of our Lord Jesus Christ, which was shed for you, preserve you blameless unto everlasting life. Drink this, in remembrance that Christ's blood was shed for you, and be thankful.

After all have partaken, the minister may then offer a concluding prayer of thanksgiving and commitment.

BENEDICTION

John Wesley's Covenant Service[16]

An Introduction

To John Wesley, founder of Methodism and principal human motivation behind the great revival that swept England and Wales in the 18th century, one means of "increasing serious religion" was the joining of believers in a covenant "to serve God with all our heart and with all our soul." He urges Methodists to renew, "at every point, our Covenant, that the Lord should be our God."

The word *covenant* has rich meaning throughout the Bible. (See Gen. 2:16-17; 6:18; 1 Sam. 18:3; Pss. 25:10; 103:18; Jer. 50:5; Matt. 26:28; Acts 3:25; Rom. 11:26-27; Heb. 7:22.) According to most contemporary dictionaries, *covenant* denotes a solemn and binding agreement; a contract; a promise between two or more parties.

When filtered through the light of God's Word and religious experience, the term *covenant* becomes a binding agreement between God and man, a promise that is dependent one upon the other. Throughout the Old Testament, and continuing into the New, God made a promise (a commitment) of continual life and favor to man on condition of obedience, coupled with a penalty for disobedience.

On August 11, 1755, John Wesley refers to an occasion when he conducted a service that provided opportunity for making or renewing individual covenants with God. At the close of that 6 P.M. meeting in the French Church in Spitalfields "all the people stood up, in testimony of assent, to the number of about 1,800 persons." The *Journal* entry closes with "such a night I scarce ever saw before. Surely the fruit of it shall remain for ever."

The success of this Covenant Service encouraged Wesley to have it published as a pamphlet in 1780. It was in this form that the service received wide distribution and use for nearly a century.

As the Church has come to recognize the value of greater congregational involvement and participation in public worship, the need for providing meaningful opportunities for making and expressing one's personal covenant relationship with God has come to the forefront. Such a need resulted in the rediscovery, by churches of varied worship traditions, of the beauty and scriptural authority contained in Wesley's original Covenant Service.

This abridged and edited version is closely based on the spirit and text of the 1780 version. It retains much of the author's language, but it veers from the original in that it suggests specific hymn selections, which are found in this volume.

To all who participate in a worship service based on this material, or who make use of it for personal devotional reading, may this historical connection with the Wesleyan Church and teaching be a reminder of our natural condition as sinners and our responsibility to reaffirm a personal covenant relationship with God. It should also provide for a renewed realization of God's promises and presence.

Suggested Use of the Covenant Service

It was John Wesley's traditional practice to make use of the Covenant Service for Watch Night or on the first Sunday of the year. These continue to be viable options. Churches may also wish to consider using it on what has become Aldersgate Sunday in Methodist churches. Isolated portions may be selected for use in other contexts, such as for reading or congregational meditation, and there is a wealth of material here for private devotional use.

For some modern worshipers, especially those of the evangelical and nonliturgical tradition, such a structured service may at first appear to be a hindrance to true worship; but as the scriptural allusions are understood, hymns sung within the context of the service, prayers prayed earnestly, and the minister's exhortations delivered with personal conviction and unction, there will be an awareness on the part of the participants of the value of this traditional service. It will be beneficial to print all portions of the service, except for the minister's exhortation, in the worship folder.

The Service

INSTRUMENTAL PRELUDE

Minister: "Come, let us join ourselves to the LORD in an everlasting covenant which will never be forgotten" (Jer. 50:5, RSV).

HYMN: "Rejoice, the Lord Is King"

Minister: Almighty God, unto whom all hearts are open, all desires known, and from whom no secrets are hid; cleanse the thoughts of our hearts by the inspiration of Thy Holy Spirit, that we may perfectly love Thee, and worthily magnify Thy holy name through Christ our Lord. Amen.

Then shall follow the minister and people praying together.

Minister and People: The Lord's Prayer (Matt. 6:9-13) (Use "trespasses")

THE SCRIPTURE LESSON: John 15:1-8

HYMN: "Jesus, We Look to Thee"

Minister: My dear friends, get these three principles fixed in your hearts: that things eternal are much more substantial than things temporal; that things not seen are as certain as the things that are seen; that upon your present choice de-

pends your eternal lot. Choose Christ and His
ways, and you are blessed forever; refuse, and
you are undone forever.

And then, beloved, make your choice. Turn either to the right hand or to the left; Christ with
His yoke, His cross, and His crown; or the devil
with his wealth, his pleasure, and his curse.
Then ask yourselves, "Soul, you see what is before you; what will you do? Which will you have,
either the crown or the curse? If you choose the
crown, remember that the day you take this, you
must be content to submit to the cross and yoke,
the service and sufferings of Christ, which are
linked to it. What do you say? Had you rather
take the gains and pleasures of sin and risk the
curse? Or will you yield yourself a servant to
Christ and so make sure the crown?"

Do not delay the matter. If you are unresolved,
you are resolved: if you remain undetermined for
Christ, you are determined for the devil. Therefore follow your hearts from day to day; let them
not rest till the matter be brought to an issue,
and see that you make a good choice.

Next, embark with Christ. Adventure yourselves with Him. Cast yourselves upon His righteousness. You are exiles from the presence of
God and fallen into a land of robbers and murderers. Your sins are robbers, your pleasures are
robbers, your companions in sin are robbers and
thieves. If you stay where you are, you perish.

Christ offers, if you will venture with Him, to bring you to God. Will you say now to Him, "Lord Jesus, wilt Thou undertake for me? Wilt Thou bring me to God and bring me into the land of promise? With Thee I will venture myself. I cast myself upon Thee, upon Thy blood, upon Thy righteousness."

This is coming to Christ as your Priest. And by this you now renounce your own righteousness.

Do you deeply sense your sins and misery without Christ?

CONFESSION

People: We acknowledge a deep sense of sin and misery. We see ourselves as sinners in need of a Savior. The Spirit of God has awakened us; a kind of awakening, as it were, in hell. We cry,

"Lord, what am I! What mean these legions round about me? These chains and fetters that are upon me?

"Lord, where am I! Is there no hope of escaping out of this wretched state? I am but dead, if I continue as I am. What may I do to be saved?"

Minister: Being made sensible of his sin and his danger, a sinner will look for help and deliverance, but he will look everywhere else before he looks unto Christ. Nothing will bring a sinner to Christ but absolute necessity. He will try to forsake his sins. He will go to prayers and sermons and sacraments, and search out if there be salvation in them. But all these, though they be useful in their places, are of no help. His duties cannot help him; these may be reckoned among his sins. Ordinances cannot help; these are but empty cisterns. They all tell him, "You knock at a wrong door; salvation is not in us."

Do you now utterly despair of your own goodness, or do you trust in anything but Christ?

SUPPLICATION

People: Lord, be merciful to me. What shall I do? Abide as I am I dare not, and how to help myself I know not. My praying will not help me. My hearing will not help me. If I give all my goods to the poor, if I should give my body to be burned, all this would not save my soul. Woe is me. What shall I do?

Minister: You must let your sins go. You must let your righteousness go. Christ came not to call the righteous, but sinners to repentance. He came to seek and to save them that are lost.

Friends, will you now adventure on Christ? You have this threefold assurance:

First, God's ordination. Christ is He whom God the Father hath appointed and sent into the world to save sinners. This is He whom God the Father has sealed as the Savior who is redeeming and reconciling the world to himself.

Second, God's command. This is His commandment, that we should believe on the name of His Son, Jesus Christ.

Third, the promise of God. "Behold, I lay in Sion a chief corner stone, elect, precious: and he that believeth on him shall not be confounded" (1 Pet. 2:6).

Now, having this threefold assurance of God's ordinance, command, and promise, you may now be bold to adventure on Christ and to apply yourselves to Him.

Then shall follow the minister and people praying together.

Minister and People: Lord Jesus, here I am, a lost creature, an enemy to God, under His wrath and curse. Wilt Thou, Lord, undertake for me, reconcile me to God, and save my soul? Do not, Lord, refuse me, for if Thou refuse me, to whom then shall I go?

If I had come in my own name, Thou mightest well have put me back; but since I come at the command of the Father, reject me not. Lord, help me. Lord, save me.

I come, Lord. I believe, Lord. I throw myself upon Thy grace and mercy. I cast myself upon Thy blood. Do not refuse me. I have not whither else to go. Here I will stay. On Thee I will trust and rest and venture myself. On Thee I lay my hope for pardon, for life, for salvation. If I perish,

I perish on Thy shoulders. If I sink, I sink in Thy vessel. If I die, I die at Thy door. Bid me not go away, for I will not go.

COMMITMENT

Minister: Yield yourselves now to the Lord. As His servants, give up the dominion and government of yourselves to Christ. "Neither yield ye your members as instruments of unrighteousness unto sin: but yield yourselves unto God, as those that are alive from the dead, and your members as instruments of righteousness unto God." "To whom ye yield yourselves servants to obey, his servants ye are to whom ye obey" (Rom. 6:13, 16). Yield yourselves so to the Lord that you may henceforth be the Lord's.

Those that yield themselves to sin and the world, their hearts say, "Sin, I am yours; World, I am yours; Riches, I am yours; Pleasures, I am yours."

Rather, with the psalmist, we say to the Lord.

Then shall minister and people affirm together.

Minister and People: I am Thine; I reverence Thee. I dedicate myself to Thy service.

Minister: In so giving yourselves to the Lord, you affirm that you will be heartily contented that He appoint you to your work.

Let Him appoint you to your work. Christ has

many services to be done; some are more easy and honorable, others more difficult and menial.

Some are suitable to our inclinations and interest; others are contrary to both. In some, we may please Christ and please ourselves, as when He requires us to feed and clothe ourselves. Indeed, there are some spiritual duties that are more pleasing than others; as to rejoice in the Lord, to be blessing and praising of God. These are the sweet works of a Christian. But then there are other works, wherein we cannot please Christ but by denying ourselves, as in bearing and forbearing, reproving men for their sins, withdrawing from their company; witnessing against their wickedness; confessing Christ and His name, when it will cost us shame and reproach; sailing against the wind, swimming against the tide, parting with our liberties and accommodations for the name of our Lord Jesus Christ.

See what it is that Christ expects and then yield yourselves to His whole will. Do not think of making your own terms with Christ; that will never be allowed you. Let us now approach Christ in prayer.

The people will join the minister in praying.

Minister and People: Lord Jesus, if Thou wilt receive me into Thy house, if Thou wilt but own me as Thy servant, I will not stand upon terms. Impose on me what condition Thou pleasest;

write down Thy own articles; command me what Thou wilt; let me be Thy servant.

Make me what Thou wilt, Lord, and set me where Thou wilt. Let me be a vessel of silver or gold, or a vessel of wood or stone; so I be a vessel of honor. I am content. If I be not the head or the eye or the ear, one of the nobler and more honorable instruments Thou wilt employ, let me be the hand or the foot, as one of the lowest and least esteemed of all the servants of my Lord.

Minister: Lord, put me to what Thou wilt; rank me with whom Thou wilt.

People: Put me to doing; put me to suffering.

Minister: Let me be employed for Thee, or laid aside for Thee, exalted for Thee, or trodden under foot for Thee.

People: Let me be full; let me be empty.

Minister: Let me have all things; let me have nothing.

People: I freely and heartily resign all to Thy pleasure and disposal.

HYMN: "Lord, in the Strength of Grace"

Minister: Beloved, such a commitment to Christ as you have now made is that wherein the essence of Christianity lies. When you have chosen God to be your portion and happiness; when you have laid all your hopes upon Christ, casting yourself wholly upon the merits of His righteousness; when you have understandingly and heartily resigned and given up yourselves to Him; then you are Christians indeed, and never till then. Christ will be the Savior of none but of His servants. He is the Author of eternal salvation to those who obey Him. Christ will have no servants but by consent. His people are a willing people, and Christ will accept of no consent but in full to all that He requires. He will be all in all, or He will be nothing.

THE COVENANT

Minister: And now let us confirm our commitment by a solemn covenant, beginning with the singing of a covenant hymn.

HYMN: "Come, Let Us Use the Grace Divine"

Minister: Search your hearts whether you either have already or can now freely make this commitment to God in Christ. First, consider what your sins are and examine whether you can resolve to forego them all. Consider what the laws are, how holy, strict, and spiritual, and whether you can, upon deliberation, make choice of them all as the rule of your whole life.

Second, compose your spirits into the most serious frame possible, suitable to a transaction of so high importance.

Third, lay hold on the covenant of God and rely upon His promise of giving grace and strength, whereby you may be enabled to perform your promise. Trust not to your own strength, but take hold on His strength.

Fourth, resolve to be faithful. Having engaged your hearts, opened your mouths, and subscribed with your hands to the Lord, resolve in His strength never to go back.

Last, being thus prepared, in the most solemn manner possible, as if the Lord were visibly present before your eyes, bow and open your hearts to the Lord.

The minister and people will bow and pray together.

Minister and People: O most holy God, I beseech Thee, accept the poor prodigal prostrating himself at Thy door. I have fallen from Thee by my iniquity and am by nature a son of death and a thousandfold more the child of hell by my wicked practice. But of Thy infinite grace Thou hast promised mercy to me in Christ if I will but turn to Thee with all my heart. Therefore upon the call of Thy gospel, I am now come and, throwing down my weapons, submit myself to Thy mercy.

And because Thou requirest, as the condition of my peace with Thee, that I should put away my idols and be at defiance with all Thy enemies, I here from the bottom of my heart renounce them all. I firmly covenant with Thee not to allow myself in any known sin, but conscientiously to use all the means that I know Thou hast prescribed, for the death and utter destruction of all my corruptions. I humbly affirm before Thy glorious Majesty that it is the firm resolution of my heart to forsake all that is dear unto me in this world, rather than to turn from Thee to the ways of sin. I will watch against all its temptations, whether of prosperity or adversity, lest they should withdraw my heart from Thee.

And since Thou hast, of Thy boundless mercy, offered graciously to me to be my God through Christ, I call heaven and earth to record this day, that I do here solemnly acknowledge Thee as the Lord my God. I do here take Thee, the Lord Jehovah, Father, Son, and Holy Ghost, for my portion and do give up myself, body and soul, for Thy servant, promising and vowing to serve Thee in holiness and righteousness all the days of my life.

O blessed Jesus, I come to Thee hungry, wretched, miserable, blind, and naked, unworthy to wash the feet of the servants of my Lord, much less to be solemnly married to the King of Glory. But since such is Thy unparalleled love, I do here with all my power accept Thee and take Thee for my Head and Husband, to love, honor, and obey Thee before all others, and this to the death. I renounce my own worthiness and do here avow Thee for the Lord my righteousness. I renounce my own wisdom and do here take Thee for my only Guide. I renounce my own will and take Thy will for my law.

And since Thou hast told me I must suffer if I will reign, I do here covenant with Thee to take my lot, as it falls, with Thee and by Thy grace to run all hazards with Thee, purposing that neither life nor death shall part between Thee and me.

Now, Almighty God, Searcher of Hearts, Thou knowest that I make this covenant with Thee this day, without any known guile or reservation, beseeching Thee that if Thou seest any flaw or falsehood therein, Thou wouldst reveal it to me and help me to put it right.

HYMN: "Father, Son, and Holy Ghost"

All shall stand and say:

Minister and People: And now, glory be to Thee, O God the Father, whom I shall be bold from this day forward to look upon as my God and Father. Glory be to Thee, O God the Son, who hast loved me and washed me from my sins in Thy own blood and art now become my Savior and Redeemer. Glory be to Thee, O God the Holy Ghost, who by Thy almighty power has turned my heart from sin to God.

O eternal Jehovah, the Lord God Omnipotent,

Father, Son, and Holy Ghost, Thou art now become my Covenant-Friend, and I, through Thy
infinite grace, am become Thy Covenant-Servant.
And the Covenant which I have made on earth,
let it be ratified in heaven. Amen.

Now may follow the Holy Communion, or a hymn may
be sung and the benediction given.

OPTIONAL HYMN: "Ye Servants of God"

Calls to Worship and Benedictions[17]

1. BIBLICAL CALLS TO WORSHIP
New International Version

"Love the LORD, all his saints! The LORD preserves the faithful. . . . Be strong and take heart, all you who hope in the LORD" (Ps. 31:23-24, all NIV, 1-2A).

"I will extol the LORD at all times; his praise will always be on my lips. My soul will boast in the LORD; let the afflicted hear and rejoice. Glorify the LORD with me; let us exalt his name together" (Ps. 34:1-3).

"Who, O God, is like you? . . . I will praise you . . . for your faithfulness, O my God; I will sing praise to you . . . I, whom you have redeemed. My tongue will tell of your righteous acts all day long" (Ps. 71:19, 22-24).

"Come, let us sing for joy to the LORD. . . . Let us come before him with thanksgiving and extol him with music and song. . . . Come, let us bow down in worship, let us kneel before the LORD our Maker" (Ps. 95:1-2, 6).

"Sing to the LORD a new song, for he has done marvelous things. . . . Shout for joy to the LORD, all the earth, burst into jubilant song with music . . . and the sound of singing" (Ps. 98:1, 4-5).

"Shout for joy to the LORD, all the earth. Worship the LORD with gladness; come before him with joyful songs. . . . Enter his gates with thanksgiving . . . and praise his name" (Ps. 100:1-2, 4).

"Praise the LORD . . . and forget not all his benefits—who forgives all your sins and heals all your diseases . . . who satisfies your desires with good things so that your youth is renewed like the eagle's. . . . The LORD is compassionate and gracious. . . . From everlasting to everlasting the LORD's love is with those who fear him. . . . Praise the LORD" (Ps. 103:2-3, 5, 8, 17, 22).

"Praise the LORD. . . . I will praise the LORD all my life; I will sing praise to my God as long as I live. . . . Blessed is he . . . whose hope is in the LORD his God, . . . the LORD, who remains faithful forever" (Ps. 146:1-2, 5-6).

"Praise the LORD. Praise God in his sanctuary. . . . Praise him for his acts of power. . . . Praise him with . . . the trumpet, praise him with the harp and lyre. . . . Let everything that has breath praise the LORD" (Ps. 150:1-3, 6).

2. BIBLICAL BENEDICTIONS AND BLESSINGS

A. *New International Version*

"May the LORD keep watch between you and me when we are away from each other" (Gen. 31:49).

"The LORD bless you and keep you; the LORD make his face shine upon you and be gracious to you; the LORD turn his face toward you and give you peace" (Num. 6:24-26).

"Love the LORD your God . . . walk in all his ways . . . obey his commands . . . hold fast to him . . . serve him with all your heart and all your soul" (Josh. 22:5).

"Praise be to the LORD, the God of Israel, from everlasting to everlasting. Amen and Amen" (Ps. 41:13).

"Praise be to the LORD God, the God of Israel, who alone does marvelous deeds. Praise be to his glorious name forever; may the whole earth be filled with his glory. Amen and Amen" (Ps. 72:18-19).

"Praise be to the LORD forever! Amen and Amen" (Ps. 89:52).

"Praise be to the LORD, the God of Israel, from everlasting to everlasting. Let all the people say, 'Amen!' Praise the LORD" (Ps. 106:48).

"Therefore go and make disciples . . . baptizing them in the name of the Father and of the Son and of the Holy Spirit, and teaching them to obey everything [Jesus has] commanded you" (Matt. 28:19-20).

"Grace and peace to you from God our Father and from the Lord Jesus Christ" (Rom. 1:7).

"Oh, the depth of the riches of the wisdom and knowledge of God! How unsearchable his judgments, and his paths beyond tracing out! . . . For from him and through him and to him are all things. To him be the glory forever! Amen" (Rom. 11:33, 36).

"For us there is but one God, the Father, from whom all things came and for whom we live; and there is but one Lord, Jesus Christ, through whom all things came and through whom we live" (1 Cor. 8:6).

"Praise be to the God and Father of our Lord Jesus Christ, the Father of compassion and the God of all comfort, who comforts us in all our troubles, so that we can comfort those in any trouble with the comfort we ourselves have received from God" (2 Cor. 1:3-4).

"May the grace of the Lord Jesus Christ, and the love of God, and the fellowship of the Holy Spirit be with you all" (2 Cor. 13:14).

"Grace and peace to you from God our Father and the Lord Jesus Christ, who gave himself for our sins to rescue us from the present evil age, according to the will of our God and Father, to whom be glory for ever and ever. Amen" (Gal. 1:3-5).

"Carry each other's burdens, and in this way you will fulfill the law of Christ. . . . Therefore, as we have opportunity, let us do good to all people, especially to those who belong to the family of believers" (Gal. 6:2, 10).

"The grace of our Lord Jesus Christ be with your spirit, brothers. Amen" (Gal. 6:18).

"Grace and peace to you from God our Father and the Lord Jesus Christ" (Eph. 1:2).

"Now to him who is able to do immeasurably more than all we ask or imagine, according to his power that is at work within us, to him be glory in the church and in Christ Jesus throughout all generations, for ever and ever! Amen" (Eph. 3:20-21).

"Peace to the brothers, and love with faith from God the Father and the Lord Jesus Christ. Grace to all who love our Lord Jesus Christ with an undying love" (Eph. 6:23-24).

"And [may] the peace of God, which transcends all understanding, . . . guard your hearts and your minds in Christ Jesus" (Phil. 4:7).

"To our God and Father be glory for ever and ever. Amen" (Phil. 4:20).

"The grace of the Lord Jesus Christ be with your spirit. Amen" (Phil. 4:23).

"May the Lord make your love increase and overflow for each other and for everyone else, just as ours does for you. May he strengthen your hearts so that you will be blameless and holy in the presence of our God and Father when our Lord Jesus comes with all his holy ones" (1 Thess. 3:12-13).

"May God himself, the God of peace, sanctify you through and through. May your whole spirit, soul and body be kept blameless at the coming of our Lord Jesus Christ. . . . The grace of our Lord Jesus Christ be with you" (1 Thess. 5:23, 28).

"May our Lord Jesus Christ himself and God our Father, who loved us and by his grace gave us eternal encouragement and good hope, encourage your hearts and strengthen you in every good deed and word" (2 Thess. 2:16-17).

"May the Lord direct your hearts into God's love and Christ's perseverance" (2 Thess. 3:5).

"Grace, mercy and peace from God the Father and Christ Jesus our Lord" (1 Tim. 1:2).

"Now to the King eternal, immortal, invisible, the only God, be honor and glory for ever and ever. Amen" (1 Tim. 1:17).

"Grace and peace from God the Father and Christ Jesus our Savior" (Titus 1:4).

"And the God of all grace, who called you to his eternal glory in Christ, after you have suffered a little while, will himself restore you and make you strong, firm and steadfast. To him be the power for ever and ever. Amen" (1 Pet. 5:10-11).

"Grace and peace be yours in abundance through the knowledge of God and of Jesus our Lord" (2 Pet. 1:2).

"To the only God our Savior be glory, majesty, power and authority, through Jesus Christ our Lord, before all ages, now and forevermore! Amen" (Jude 25).

"Worthy is the Lamb, who was slain, to receive power and wealth and wisdom and strength and honor and glory and praise! . . . To him who sits on the throne and to the Lamb be praise and honor and glory and power, for ever and ever! . . . Amen" (Rev. 5:12-14).

B. *King James Version*

"The LORD our God be with us, as he was with our fathers: let him not leave us, nor forsake us: that he may incline our hearts unto him, to walk in all his ways, and to keep his commandments, and his statutes, and his judgments, which he commanded our fathers" (1 Kings 8:57-58).

"Let the words of my mouth, and the meditation of my heart, be acceptable in thy sight, O LORD, my strength, and my redeemer" (Ps. 19:14).

"Now the God of hope fill you with all joy and peace in believing, that ye may abound in hope, through the power of the Holy Ghost. . . .Now the God of peace be with you all. Amen" (Rom. 15:13, 33).

"The grace of our Lord Jesus Christ be with you all. Amen" (Rom. 16:24).

"Now to him that is of power to stablish you according to my gospel, and the preaching of Jesus Christ, according to the revelation of the mystery, which was kept secret since the world began, but now is made manifest, and by the scriptures of the prophets, according to the commandment of the everlasting God, made known to all nations for the obedience of faith: to God only wise, be glory through Jesus Christ for ever. Amen" (Rom. 16:25-27).

"Grace be unto you, and peace, from God our Father, and from the Lord Jesus Christ" (1 Cor. 1:3).

"Be perfect, be of good comfort, be of one mind, live in peace; and the God of love and peace shall be with you. . . . The grace of the Lord Jesus

Christ, and the love of God, and the communion of the Holy [Spirit], be with you all. Amen" (2 Cor. 13:11, 14).

"Peace be to the brethren, and love with faith, from God the Father and the Lord Jesus Christ. Grace be with all them that love our Lord Jesus Christ in sincerity. Amen" (Eph. 6:23-24).

"Wherefore also we pray always for you, that our God would count you worthy of this calling, and fulfill all the good pleasure of his goodness, and the work of faith with power: that the name of our Lord Jesus Christ may be glorified in you, and ye in him, according to the grace of our God and the Lord Jesus Christ" (2 Thess. 1:11-12).

"Now the Lord of peace himself give you peace always by all means. The Lord be with you all. . . . The grace of our Lord Jesus Christ be with you all. Amen" (2 Thess. 3:16, 18).

"Now the God of peace, that brought again from the dead our Lord Jesus, that great shepherd of the sheep, through the blood of the everlasting covenant, make you perfect in every good work to do his will, working in you that which is wellpleasing in his sight, through Jesus Christ; to whom be glory for ever and ever. Amen" (Heb. 13:20-21).

"Grace be with you, mercy, and peace, from God

the Father, and from the Lord Jesus Christ, the Son of the Father, in truth and love" (2 John 3).

"Now unto him that is able to keep you from falling, and to present you faultless before the presence of his glory with exceeding joy, to the only wise God our Saviour, be glory and majesty, dominion and power, both now and ever. Amen" (Jude 24-25).

"Grace be unto you, and peace, from him which is, and which was, and which is to come; and from the seven Spirits which are before his throne; and from Jesus Christ, who is the faithful witness, and the first begotten of the dead, and the prince of the kings of the earth. Unto him that loved us, and washed us from our sins in his own blood, and hath made us kings and priests unto God and his Father; to him be glory and dominion for ever and ever. Amen" (Rev. 1:4-6).

3. OTHER BENEDICTIONS

Now may you continue to grow in the grace and knowledge of our Lord Jesus Christ, feeding on His Word, breathing in His Spirit, walking in His light, resting on His promises.

May His Spirit dwell within you, His Word abide in you, His will guide you, His joy strengthen you as you give Him your lives in loving service. Amen.

Go in peace. May you be constantly comforted by the thought that God loves you and wants you to be like Him through the power of the Holy Spirit. Amen.

Unto God's gracious mercy and protection we commit you; the Lord look upon you with His favor and fill you with all spiritual benediction and peace; that in this life, and in the world to come, you may be partakers of eternal grace, through Jesus Christ our Lord.

Go in peace; sin no more. Love one another.

May the same Spirit that settled upon the 120 on the Day of Pentecost energize you as you leave this church to serve in the world. Amen.

Lean thine arms upon the windowsill of heaven and gaze upon the Lord—then go out to meet thy day.

Offertory Ideas and Prayers[18]

1. OFFERTORY IDEA

A senator's wife went into the ham business—no pun intended. She borrowed $100,000 for capital from a trust company. The business finally made $3 million in annual sales.

The chairman of the trust company said to the senator, "I'm glad the ham venture is doing well."

The senator asked, "What makes you think it's doing well?"

The chairman replied, "You used to call it 'Betty's business.' Now you call it 'our business.'"

That's not far off from church business. Nontithers call it "their church." Tithers lovingly refer to it as "our church."

Offertory Prayer

DEAR FATHER: Grant us grace to heed the word of praise or warning from Your Son: "Where your treasure is, there will your heart be also." In Jesus' name, Amen.

2. OFFERTORY IDEA

A pastor was speaking to the Sunday School about the things money can't buy. "It can't buy laughter, and it can't buy love," he told them. Driving his point home, he said, "What would you do if I offered you $1,000 not to love your mother and father?"

Stunned silence followed. Finally, a small voice

asked, "How much would you give me not to love my big sister?"

Giving is not loving, but we can't love without giving!

Offertory Prayer

DEAR FATHER: We've discovered that Christian growth does not come by pouring in but by giving out! Accept our gifts of love. In Jesus' name, Amen.

3. OFFERTORY IDEA

An old radio recording of Amos 'n' Andy had an interesting conversation. Amos 'n' Andy were talking about finance.

Amos said to Andy: "Andy, if you got money, you can do business. If you don't, you gotta make arrangements."

Tithing is the best financial arrangement God has set up for developing Christian character and opportunities for learning to depend on Him.

Offertory Prayer

DEAR FATHER:
The more we give, the more we get;
The more we laugh, the less we fret;
The more we do unselfishly,
The more we love abundantly;
The more of everything we share,
The more we show how much we care;
The more we love, the more we'll find

That life is good and friends are kind;
For only what we give away
Enriches us from day to day.
In Jesus' name, Amen.

4. OFFERTORY IDEA

It's been said in these economic times that the way to stay in the black today is to make and sell red ink.

Said the robin to the sparrow, "I should really like to know

Why these anxious human beings rush about and worry so."

Said the sparrow to the robin, "Friend, I think that it must be

That they have no Heavenly Father such as cares for you and me."

Offertory Prayer

DEAR FATHER: Please remind us that our individual stewardship is what we do after we have said, "I believe." In Jesus' name, Amen.

5. OFFERTORY IDEA

A writer was attempting to reconstruct the life of the Duke of Wellington in order to write a biography. The author said he learned most by finding an old account book of Wellington's. From it he learned how the great man spent his money.

The researcher thought the old account book of Wellington's spending taught him more about the man than reading speeches about the duke or even his own public pronouncements.

The way a man spends his money indicates what he thinks is important in life.

Offertory Prayer
> *Not what I get, but what I give —*
> *This be the gauge by which I live.*
> *Not merely joys that come my way,*
> *But the help I give to those astray.*
> *Not the rewards of money and fame,*
> *But the loads I lift in Jesus' name.*
> *This be the pay at the end of the day —*
> *Not what I keep, but give away.*
> In Jesus' name, Amen.

6. OFFERTORY IDEA

A state senator from Pennsylvania argued that his constituents were so drained financially, they simply could not afford to pay another cent in taxes.

In his oratory, he cited a letter from an irate voter as proof. The citizen had written him to protest higher taxes, insisting their family could not possibly pay any more. In fact, she pointed out, they already paid the government income taxes and sales taxes—and besides, they bought licenses for their two cars, summer camper, houseboat, and motorboat!

I wonder if that's how we sometimes sound to

God when we declare we just can't afford to obey Him by tithing our income. I doubt God laughs about it.

Offertory Prayer
> *We mustn't boast how much we are giving*
> > *Until we've given Your part.*
> *Our tithe comes out of our wallet;*
> > *Our offering comes from our heart.*

In Jesus' name, Amen.

7. OFFERTORY IDEA

A young woman was selling tickets for an upcoming charity concert. She had approached a well-known man of the community about buying some tickets for the charity event.

Politely but firmly he replied, "I'm sorry, but I won't be able to attend the concert. I know it's for a worthy cause. However, I'll assure you I shall be with you in spirit."

The young woman brilliantly exclaimed, "Fine! And where would you like to have your spirit sit? In the $5 section or the $10 section?"

Meekly, the gentleman replied: "I'll take a $10 ticket, please."

Now I know we are entering into the summer vacation season. I expect you all to get a good vacation away from responsibilities and pressure. I know you'll be with us in spirit!

And don't forget to have your spirit tithe regularly while you are on vacation.

Offertory Prayer

DEAR JESUS: We learned an important lesson by Your example: Worship without sacrifice is an impossibility! Amen.

8. OFFERTORY IDEA

The parish priest of Moncontour, France, looked at the meager offering in the collection plate. The coins didn't even cover the bottom.

The priest turned to his congregation and declared, "My brothers and sisters, earlier today, when I arrived at church, I saw all those fine cars parked in the square. I asked myself, Where are the poor? Now, having seen the collection basket, I wonder, Where are the rich?"

We'll find it better to be rich in God's eyes than rich in men's eyes. Men count dollars; God checks percentages! He asks 10 percent for the privilege of stewardship.

Offertory Prayer

DEAR HEAVENLY FATHER: We speak about stewardship—yet we know we should talk more about Lordship. When we are right on the Lordship of Jesus, we'll be right in our stewardship. Our pocketbooks will fall in line when we really learn that we are not our own but have been bought with a price! In Jesus' name, Amen.

9. OFFERTORY IDEA

Two preachers were discussing the financial

situation of their churches. The holiness preacher, whose congregation numbered about 100, mentioned the amount of total giving by his church for the past year.

The other, pastor of a liberal church that ran three Sunday morning services totaling around 900, was astounded. The flabbergasted minister stated, "Your little church takes in more money than my big church!" Wistfully he added, "If it weren't for the bingo parties, our church would never make it. How do you people do it?"

The simple reply, "My people practice tithing!"

Tithing is the Bible method of support and the Bible method of developing strong, obedient stewards whom God can bless!

Offertory Prayer

DEAR HEAVENLY FATHER: Help us give according to our incomes, lest You make our incomes match our gifts! In Jesus' name, Amen.

10. OFFERTORY IDEA

One summer Monday night, I got to attend the opening exhibition game of the Los Angeles Rams in Anaheim Stadium. They played against —and lost to—the New England Patriots.

Standing in line to get a supper of Coke and a very dry hot dog, I heard a lot of grumbling from the patrons of the Rams. People who had good seats at the Coliseum for more than 30 years had been assigned poor seats in Anaheim. That set up a mood of complaint. Many said they were going to quit going to the Rams' football games.

Here are some of the reasons given for staying home:

(1) The stadium has gotten so large that I don't see any of the old-time fans anymore. No one ever speaks to me.

(2) Game day is the only day I have to sleep.

(3) Often we have guests—and then other times we go to the cabin.

(4) The seats are hard.

(5) The coach never comes to call on me. He doesn't even recognize me on the street.

(6) The band and the cheerleaders use new tunes and yells. I like the old pep tunes better.

(7) There are some people in the stands who are hypocrites. Most of them just come to be seen by the TV cameras.

(8) I saw too many games as a child. My parents forced me to go.

(9) I can watch on TV without getting involved.

(10) They always have their hands out for money. I have to pay for a ticket every time I come.

Offertory Prayer

DEAR FATHER: In Your Book we discover a consistent principle: No man is really consecrated until his money is dedicated. In Jesus' name, Amen.

11. OFFERTORY IDEAS

Someone gave me a cartoon from *Family Circus*. Several little children were seated on stools and the floor, one boy was standing up on a low table with a book in hand, and a little girl had pulled out a breadbasket from Mother's cupboard. She was saying, "Mommy, can we use this basket? We're playing church!"

Children learn to mimic at an early age. In those years they are open to our values.

Bonnie had come home from a church service where the pastor had been raising pledges for a revival meeting. When her mother couldn't find her after dinner, she went looking. At last she found Bonnie in the chicken house with several hens cornered. She was saying to them, "Every one of you hens that'll promise to lay an egg today hold up your hand!"

Adult attitudes toward stewardship shape the attitude of children toward spiritual values. Are our habits worth mimicking?

Offertory Prayer
DEAR HEAVENLY FATHER:

Your plan shows wisdom much higher than ours, because:

> What I kept I lost.
> What I spent I had.
> What I gave I have!
> In Jesus' name, Amen.

Notes

1. J. Kenneth Grider, *A Wesleyan-Holiness Theology* (Kansas City: Beacon Hill Press of Kansas City, 1994), 502-3.

2. *Manual, 1993-1997: Church of the Nazarene* (Kansas City: Nazarene Publishing House), 28.

3. Rob L. Staples, *Outward Sign and Inward Grace* (Kansas City: Beacon Hill Press of Kansas City, 1991), 179-80.

4. H. Ray Dunning, *Grace, Faith, and Holiness* (Kansas City: Beacon Hill Press of Kansas City, 1988), 550.

5. Staples, *Outward Sign and Inward Grace,* 180.

6. Ibid.

7. Adapted from Manfred Holck Jr., *Dedication Services for All Occasions* (Valley Forge, Pa.: Judson Press, 1984), 39.

8. Ibid., 91-92.

9. Adapted from "The Hanging of the Greens" by Sally Rhodes Ahner. Copyright © 1986 by Abingdon Press. Used by permission.

10. Excerpts from *The Book of Blessings*, additional blessings for use in the United States of America. Copyright © 1988 United States Catholic Conference, Washington, D.C. Adapted and used with permission of the copyright owner. All rights reserved.

11. Ibid.

12. Adapted from *From Hope to Joy*, Don E. Saliers. Copyright © 1984 by Abingdon Press. Used by permission.

13. James R. Spruce, ed., *A Pastor's Worship Resource—for Advent, Lent, and Other Occasions* (Kansas City: Beacon Hill Press of Kansas City, 1987), 67-74.

14. Ibid., 123-33.

15. Prayer by Michael J. O'Donnell, *The United Methodist Book of Worship*. Copyright © 1992 by The United Methodist Publishing House. Used by permission.

16. Ken Bible, comp., *Wesley Hymns* (Kansas City: Lillenas Publishing Co., 1982), A-2-10.

17. Spruce, *Pastor's Worship Resource,* 175-82.

18. Ibid., 183-90.

Rituals/Ceremonies in *Manual*/1993-97 Church of the Nazarene

For ministers and worship leaders who use the *Manual of the Church of the Nazarene,* the following rituals in this book may be found as numbered in that source: